AVOIDANT A STYLE RECOVERY

BREAK FREE FROM FEAR, REWIRE YOUR MIND,

AND BUILD SECURE RELATIONSHIPS

RICHARD BANKS

3

Why You Should Read This Book

Do you crave intimacy but feel overwhelmed when someone gets too close? Are you torn between wanting love and protecting your independence? Do you withdraw when emotions rise, leaving you feeling misunderstood or emotionally drained? Or are you in a relationship with someone who struggles to open up, commit, or show affection?"

If this sounds familiar, you're not alone—and the good news is, it doesn't have to be this way. **Avoidant attachment is more common than you think**, and while it may feel like an unchangeable part of who you are, it doesn't have to be your destiny.

It's time to break free from the cycle of avoidance and step into secure, lasting love.

In **Avoidant Attachment Style Recovery**, relationship coach **Richard Banks** offers a proven, step-by-step guide to break free from the chains of

5

avoidance and step into the fulfilling relationships you've always dreamed of. This is more than a self-help book—it's a **practical toolkit, grounded in attachment theory and psychology-backed research**, designed to empower you to transform your relationship patterns for good.

Inside, you'll discover:

- How to stop pushing people away and rewire your response to intimacy.
- How childhood shapes avoidant behaviors—and how to break free from these patterns.
- Step-by-step strategies to move toward **secure attachment—without losing your independence.**
- How to **communicate without fear** and navigate emotional conversations with confidence.
- How to **repair trust and intimacy**—whether you're in a relationship or working toward one.
- Ways to **heal past relationship wounds** and stop repeating destructive patterns.

This book is for you if:

- You've been called emotionally unavailable, distant, or hard to read.
- You find yourself pushing people away when things get too close.
- You want love, but commitment feels overwhelming or suffocating.
- You feel "stuck" in relationships, struggling to balance independence with intimacy.
- You're in a relationship with an avoidant partner and want to understand their behavior and build a stronger bond..

Backed by research and packed with real-life solutions, this book goes beyond theory—it provides **case studies, exercises, and actionable insights** to make transformation practical and achievable. Written with **deep empathy and understanding**, it meets you where you are without judgment, guiding you gently toward healing and growth.

You don't have to stay stuck in the cycle of avoidance. Whether you're single, in a relationship, or seeking to understand your avoidant partner,

Avoidant Attachment Style Recovery will guide you every step of the way.

Stop settling for less. Take the first step toward secure, fulfilling relationships today. **Click 'Buy Now' and start your transformation**—because you deserve a love that feels safe, deep, and lasting!

Thank You!

Thank you for your purchase.

I am dedicated to making the most enriching and informational content. I hope it meets your expectations and you gain a lot from it.

Your comments and feedback are important to me because they help me to provide the best material possible. So, if you have any questions or concerns, please email me at richard@richardbanks.cc

Again, thank you for your purchase.

INTRODUCTION

"The walls we build around us to keep sadness out also keep out the joy." – Jim Rohn

Have you ever experienced that strong desire to be close to others while also feeling an instinctive fear of it? Do you push people away despite their attempts to show you love? Or perhaps you've been told you're "too independent" or "emotionally unavailable," yet the thought of depending on someone else makes you feel uneasy.

If any of this sounds familiar, you're not alone. Research reveals that around 25% of people have an avoidant attachment style. This style is often rooted in childhood experiences, resulting in challenges with emotional intimacy, a fierce need for independence, and difficulty investing time and energy in relationships. But here's the empowering truth: while these patterns might feel like an unchangeable part of who you are, they are not your destiny.

Attachment theory, developed by British psychologist John Bowlby, provides a framework for understanding the emotional bonds we form with others. Initially created to study the relationships between children and their caregivers, attachment theory has since expanded to encompass adult relationships, particularly romantic ones.

According to this theory, everyone is born with an innate need to bond with others. These bonds influence how we experience love, connection, and intimacy throughout our lives. Attachment theory identifies four primary attachment styles: secure, avoidant, anxious, and disorganized. For individuals with an avoidant attachment style, emotional closeness often feels overwhelming. They use their independence as a shield, even if it means sacrificing meaningful connections with others.

Your attachment style is like a default setting for how you approach love and relationships. It influences your choice of partners, shapes how you interpret feelings of love, and dictates how you respond to intimacy. For someone with avoidant attachment, love can feel like you're walking a tightrope: balancing your desire for connection with the fear of losing control or being emotionally overwhelmed.

Attachment in adulthood influences romantic relationships and how we connect with friends, family, and colleagues. It impacts how we communicate, resolve conflict, and navigate emotional highs and lows. Understanding your attachment style is the first step in transforming how you relate to yourself and others.

In relationships, avoidantly attached individuals often prioritize independence by keeping conversations superficial and focusing on work and hobbies. This is a protective response to the perceived threat of vulnerability, not a rejection of affection. However, this avoidance can lead to disconnection, loneliness, and misunderstanding, even while appearing self-sufficient. This emotional tug-of-war often creates confusion for you and those who care about you.

Your attachment style isn't something you chose. It was shaped by your early life experiences, often before you could describe your emotions. Perhaps you grew up in an environment where your emotional needs were dismissed, or maybe you were encouraged to be self-reliant to avoid "burdening" others. Over time, you learned that vulnerability felt unsafe and self-reliance was the best way to protect yourself.

Imagine a child on a playground. A securely attached child explores, knowing they can turn to their caregiver for comfort if needed. This consistent availability teaches them self-soothing and builds a sense of safety. For an avoidantly attached child, that consistent comfort was often missing due to a caregiver's emotional unavailability, dismissiveness, or inconsistency. This disruption teaches the child to suppress their emotional needs and rely solely on themselves—a strategy that, while helpful in childhood, creates barriers to forming connections in adulthood.

What if there were a way to balance your independence and still have meaningful connections? What if you could embrace emotional intimacy without losing yourself in the process? Imagine having relationships where you don't feel the constant need to guard your heart and feel safe enough to express your feelings without fear of rejection or losing control. This book offers that opportunity.

The principles and practices shared in the following pages are designed to help you break free from the emotional walls that no longer serve you. These patterns, while protective in childhood, often become barriers to connection and growth in adulthood. By addressing these deeply rooted habits, you can begin to rewrite your relationship with intimacy and trust.

You'll learn how to build stronger, more secure connections with loved ones and friends— relationships that don't feel like a threat to your autonomy but rather a source of mutual support and joy. Whether navigating the early stages of a new relationship or deepening an existing bond, this book will guide you toward balanced and fulfilling interactions.

We'll explore how to recognize and address the triggers that keep you stuck in emotional distance. From identifying the situations that make you want to retreat to understanding the thoughts fueling your avoidance, you'll develop the self-awareness needed to pause, reflect, and choose a healthier path. Instead of pulling away, you'll learn to lean into connection with confidence.

Healing your attachment wounds involves understanding how early experiences shaped your beliefs and behaviors, not reliving the past. By creating space for vulnerability and building trust in yourself and others, you can begin to shift these patterns. This journey is profoundly rewarding, leading to a life where independence coexists with deep connection. A life where you feel secure, loved, and understood—not despite who you are, but because of it. This book is your guide to making that vision a reality.

Most importantly, this book will help you reclaim your self-worth. At its core, avoidant attachment often stems from a belief that your needs aren't valid or that you are unworthy of care. Through this journey, you'll discover how to be your authentic self in all your relationships, embracing the truth that you deserve love, connection, and understanding.

Attachment theory is at the heart of this work, and its principles have guided many people toward healthier, more fulfilling relationships. As a mentor and life coach, I've witnessed firsthand the transformative power of understanding attachment styles, guiding countless individuals toward healing and secure connections. I've learned that we come by our attachment styles honestly—they are not flaws but adaptive responses to our early environments. Only when we develop an awareness of the roots of our behaviors can we begin to change them and work toward what psychologists refer to as "earned security" in our relationships.

This book is written with compassion, care, and integrity, designed to meet you wherever you are in your journey. You'll find practical exercises, case studies, and actionable strategies to help you create meaningful changes without sacrificing your independence or autonomy.

If you're reading this book because someone you care about struggles with avoidant attachment, you've likely experienced the sting of emotional distance or the frustration of being pushed away just as you're trying to draw closer. You may feel confused, hurt, or unsure how to navigate your relationship without losing yourself.

This book is also for you.

This book offers understanding, not excuses, shedding light on why these patterns exist and how they can be addressed with empathy, patience, and clear boundaries. When you recognize that avoidant behaviors often stem from a protective instinct rather than a lack of care, it becomes easier to approach the relationship with compassion while still advocating for your own needs.

You'll find insights and strategies for interacting with someone who has avoidant attachment, whether they're a romantic partner, friend, or family member.

You'll learn how to:

- Recognize the signs of avoidant attachment and what triggers emotional distancing.
- Communicate your needs clearly and constructively without inundating your loved one.
- Foster trust and connection by creating a safe, nonjudgmental space for vulnerability.
- Avoid common relational pitfalls like the "pursuer-distancer" dynamic.
- Balance supporting your loved one's healing journey with prioritizing your own emotional health.

By opening this book, you've already taken the first step. Whether you're here for yourself or someone you love, this book is designed to serve you both on your journey to connection and healing. These pages are not about judgment or blame but about growth, healing, and unlocking new possibilities. Together, we'll tackle the challenges of avoidant attachment and shine a light on the unique strengths you possess within.

Are you ready to break free from the patterns that hold you back and create a life of deeper connection, trust, and authentic self-expression? Let's take the first step together.

CHAPTER 1: LOVE ON LOCKDOWN

"It is not the walls that keep others out but the fear that resides within them." – Anonymous

Is This You?

You value your independence, often to the point of feeling that relationships are more trouble than they're worth. Even when you do connect with someone, a part of you wonders if you're truly cut out for it or if life would be easier alone.

- Do you plan an "exit strategy" when commitment is mentioned?

- Do you crave closeness yet feel trapped when it happens?
- Do you feel you have much to offer in relationships but end up feeling unfulfilled and misunderstood?
- Do you avoid conflict or tough conversations, even though it hurts your relationships?
- Do you keep things surface-level to avoid getting hurt despite feeling lonely?
- Do you push people away when they get close, believing it's better to end things before they do?
- Do you tend to attract overly critical or emotionally needy partners, reinforcing your doubts about relationships?
- Do you need lots of alone time, yet still experience emptiness from avoiding deeper connection?"

If this resonates, there's no need to blame yourself. These behaviors aren't flaws—they're protective strategies you've developed over time to feel safe. You may not have learned how to express your needs, set boundaries, or feel vulnerable with others without fear of rejection. But here's the good news: you can learn.

This chapter is here to help you understand why you feel and act this way in relationships. We'll explore the roots of avoidant attachment, what it looks like in your life, and how it shapes your experiences with intimacy. Most importantly, we'll begin to uncover a path forward—a way to break free from these patterns and create the meaningful connections you deserve.

THE ROOTS OF AVOIDANT ATTACHMENT

To understand avoidant attachment, we must first examine its origins in childhood. British psychologist John Bowlby's attachment theory suggests that the bonds we form with our caregivers early in life profoundly shape how we handle relationships as adults. These formative relationships create a blueprint for how we experience intimacy, trust, and emotional connection.

When a caregiver is consistently nurturing, responsive, and attuned to a child's needs, the child learns that the world is a safe place where their needs

29

will be met. This fosters a secure attachment style. However, when a caregiver is emotionally unavailable, dismissive, or inconsistent in their responses, the child adapts differently. They learn to rely on themselves, suppressing their emotional needs because seeking comfort or connection doesn't feel safe or reliable. Over time, this suppression becomes an automatic response to emotional discomfort—a deeply ingrained belief that "I must handle it alone; I cannot depend on others."

These early childhood experiences directly influence the development of avoidant attachment. The child learns that vulnerability is risky and that emotional needs are not consistently met. This lesson translates into adulthood as a deep-seated fear of vulnerability in relationships. Opening up to others feels dangerous because, subconsciously, closeness has been associated with the potential for disappointment or rejection.

The roots of avoidant attachment are often visible in early childhood behaviors. Imagine a child playing at the park while their parent sits nearby. Most children will occasionally look back at their parents for reassurance or seek them out if they fall and get hurt. A child with avoidant tendencies, however, might behave differently. They may prefer to play alone, avoid eye contact with their parents, and suppress any visible signs of distress, even when they are clearly upset. This isn't because they experience fewer emotions than other children; rather, they have learned that expressing those emotions doesn't consistently bring comfort or support. They have learned to self-soothe (or attempt to) from an early age.

Common signs of avoidant attachment in children include:

- **Pseudo-independence:** Preferring solitary play and minimizing engagement with caregivers.
- **Avoiding physical comfort:** Rejecting hugs, cuddles, or other forms of soothing touch, especially after experiencing pain or distress.

- **Emotional suppression:** Rarely crying, expressing sadness, or showing other signs of emotional distress.
- **Indifference after separation:** Appearing unaffected or minimally reactive when a caregiver leaves or returns.

Understanding that these behaviors don't indicate a lack of emotion is crucial. These children have simply learned to conceal their emotional needs to protect themselves from disappointment or rejection.

THE INTERNAL EXPERIENCE: WHAT AVOIDANT ATTACHMENT FEELS LIKE

For adults with avoidant attachment, relationships often feel like walking on a tightrope between craving connection and fearing the vulnerability it demands. Internally, it's an exhausting balancing act. On the one hand, you may long for closeness, but on the other, the thought of emotional dependency feels overwhelming—even threatening.

Here's a typical internal experience for avoidants:

- Desiring Closeness but Fearing It: While you want connection and intimacy, these feelings often come with discomfort, making it easier to withdraw than to reach out. This creates an internal conflict: you want closeness but fear vulnerability.
- The Fear of Dependence: You thrive on independence, taking pride in self-sufficiency. However, any perceived reliance—whether it's someone depending on you or you depending on them—can evoke feelings of being trapped and a fear of losing your freedom.
- Constant Vigilance: This fear of dependency often leads to a constant state of vigilance, scanning for signs that someone might demand more than you're willing to give, making even simple requests for reassurance feel daunting.
- Emotional Guarding: To protect yourself, you may engage in emotional guarding. Sharing your feelings—even with trusted people—can feel deeply uncomfortable, even unsafe. Instead, you keep conversations light and steer

clear of emotional depth, avoiding intimacy (both physical and emotional).

- Emotional Shutdown: When problems arise in relationships, you may shut down emotionally, convincing yourself you don't care. This emotional numbness is a way to avoid the pain of conflict or rejection.

- Escape-Readiness: This underlying anxiety can lead to a constant awareness of exit routes— emotionally or physically—and you may constantly assess when or how to leave a relationship.

This internal struggle creates a push-and-pull dynamic. You may engage just enough to keep the relationship intact but pull away whenever closeness feels overwhelming. The result is often a cycle of connection and withdrawal, leaving both you and your partner feeling unfulfilled and confused.

Outward Manifestations: What Avoidant Attachment Looks Like

At first glance, avoidant attachment might not seem like avoidance at all. Many individuals with this style

34

can be charming, attentive, and even affectionate, particularly in the early stages of a relationship. However, as emotional intimacy deepens, subtle yet significant behaviors begin to emerge—distancing tactics designed to keep vulnerability at bay. These behaviors, often subconscious, stem from the core fear of vulnerability and the associated belief that closeness equals danger. These distancing tactics are known as *deactivation strategies*: unconscious behaviors used by avoidants to cope with feelings of being overwhelmed when intimacy increases. They are methods to create emotional distance and regain a sense of control.

Here's how these internal fears and beliefs manifest externally, along with examples of deactivation strategies that reinforce these patterns:

1. Discomfort with Emotional Intimacy: Avoidants often feel uneasy when relationships move beyond a superficial level. This discomfort can manifest as:

- **Struggling to express affection or say "I love you":** Fearing the vulnerability that comes with these expressions.

  Deactivation Strategy: Being vague about their feelings for their partner.

- **Feeling panicked or suffocated when a partner seeks deeper emotional connection:** Perceiving requests for intimacy as demands for control.

  Deactivation Strategy: Pulling away after feeling incredibly close.

- **Withdrawing or deflecting during intimate moments:** Redirecting conversations or avoiding emotional topics altogether.

  Deactivation Strategy: Avoiding physical closeness.

- **Becoming uncomfortable when others share strong emotions:** Preferring light, unemotional interactions.

Deactivation Strategy: Focusing on their partner's imperfections to justify emotional distance.

2. Avoidance of Commitment and Conflict: Commitment and conflict can feel like significant threats to an avoidant's sense of control and independence. This avoidance can appear as:

- **Creating distance or delaying commitment:** Whether it's making plans or moving in together, commitment feels like a loss of freedom.

  Deactivation Strategy: Believing they aren't ready to commit, even after years with someone.

- **Avoiding conflict or difficult conversations:** Shutting down, deflecting, or physically withdrawing during disagreements.

  Deactivation Strategy: Assuming the worst about their partner's intentions during conflict.

- **Preferring casual or low-stakes relationships:** Avoiding relationships that require long-term investment or vulnerability.

  Deactivation Strategy: Being in a relationship with no foreseeable future, such as maintaining a long-distance romance without any plans to close the gap.

- **Entering relationships with built-in limitations:** Dating long-distance partners, unavailable people, or those in temporary situations.

  Deactivation Strategy: Withholding information to maintain a sense of independence and protect personal boundaries.

3. Hyper-Focus on Independence: For avoidants, independence is more than a preference; it's a core coping mechanism closely linked to their self-identity. This can be observed in:

- **Prioritizing work, hobbies, or social activities over relationships:** Viewing these as safer, more controllable outlets for their energy and attention.

  Deactivation Strategy: Overvaluing independence at the expense of meaningful connections.

- **Rejecting help or support from others:** Insisting they can handle everything independently, even when genuinely needing assistance.

  Deactivation Strategy: Focusing on their partner's imperfections to justify emotional distance.

- **Being hyper-vigilant about feeling controlled or "boxed in" by a partner:** Perceiving normal relationship dynamics as threats to their autonomy.

  Deactivation Strategy: Assuming the worst about their partner's requests for connection.

- **Valuing self-sufficiency to the point of avoiding reliance on others entirely, even when support is genuinely needed.**

  Deactivation Strategy: Relying on others can feel risky, fearing it may lead to loss of control, disappointment, or emotional entanglement.

4. Emotional Guarding and Self-Containment: Avoidants are often reluctant to reveal vulnerabilities, leading to:

- **Sharing little about themselves, even with close friends or partners:** Keeping conversations superficial and avoiding emotional depth.
- **Struggling to process or communicate emotions:** Often due to a limited emotional vocabulary and a history of suppressing feelings.
- **Suppressing feelings, leading to emotional numbness or an inability to engage deeply:** This emotional shutdown is a way to avoid the potential pain of vulnerability.

- **Withdrawing during emotional arguments or conflicts:** Becoming distant, aloof, or cold as a way to self-soothe.

5. Unrealistic Expectations and Idealization: Avoidants may create emotional distance by:

- **Having idealized notions of a "perfect" relationship or partner:** Setting impossibly high standards and being easily disappointed by real-life imperfections.

  Deactivation Strategy: Fantasizing about some ideal partner or ex-partner.

- **Finding faults or becoming overly annoyed by minor habits in their partner:** Using these flaws as justification for emotional withdrawal.

  Deactivation Strategy: Magnifying flaws by focusing on these minor imperfections to create emotional distance.

- **Idealizing past relationships or exes:** Romanticizing past connections because the distance makes them feel safe And comfortable.

Deactivation Strategy: Idealizing past relationships by using nostalgia to avoid investing in the present.

6. Push-Pull Dynamics: A hallmark of avoidant attachment is the push-pull dynamic:

- **Pushing people away when they get too close:** Only to experience a sense of loss and longing once they're gone.
- **Feeling torn between desiring connection and fearing vulnerability:** This internal conflict creates inconsistent behavior.
- **Overthinking relationships after they end but struggling to find resolution:** This rumination can prevent them from fully moving on.

7. Internal Struggles and Hidden Vulnerabilities: Beneath the confident exterior, avoidants often experience:

- **A hidden fear of being "unlovable" or a failure in relationships:** Despite projecting a strong sense of self-worth, there is a concern of being let down.
- **Overwhelmed by emotions:** Due to years of suppression, the intense feelings can be frightening.
- **Worrying that their partner will react negatively if they open up:** Leading to a reluctance to share their true feelings.

8. Loyalty and Selective Connection: Despite their challenges with intimacy, avoidants can demonstrate deep loyalty to a select few:

- **Forming strong attachments to pets:** Feels safer and less demanding than human relationships.
- **Maintaining strong bonds with a small inner circle:** Offering unwavering loyalty even while struggling with vulnerability.

9. Misinterpreting Partners' Intentions: Avoidants may misinterpret their partner's actions due to hyper-vigilance:

43

- **Assuming requests for connection are attempts to control or trap them:** This misinterpretation fuels their desire for distance.
- **Expecting negative or critical reactions if they open up:** Even when there's no evidence to support this fear.

10. Conflict Avoidance and Withdrawal: When faced with conflict, avoidants tend to:

- **Retreat emotionally or physically:** Becoming distant and unresponsive.
- **Shut down or deflect during emotionally charged situations:** Leaving their partner feeling unheard and dismissed.

It's crucial to understand that these behaviors aren't malicious. They are protective mechanisms designed to shield avoidants from the perceived pain of vulnerability. Unfortunately, these strategies can leave loved ones feeling confused, rejected, or insecure. Comprehending this connection between internal experience and external behavior fosters empathy for both avoidantly attached individuals and their partners.

DEBUNKING MISCONCEPTIONS ABOUT AVOIDANT ATTACHMENT

When it comes to avoidant attachment, there's a lot of misunderstanding—and even misinformation—out there. It's common for dismissive avoidants to be labeled as "uncaring," "selfish," or "incapable of love," but these characterizations don't paint the whole picture. Avoidant attachment is a complex, deeply human experience that stems from learned behaviors and survival strategies. By unpacking these misconceptions, we can shed light on the truth about avoidant attachment and create a more compassionate understanding of those who live with it.

- Avoidant People Don't Want Relationships

One of the most widespread myths about avoidant attachment is that avoidant people don't want relationships. This couldn't be further from the truth. Most avoidant individuals desire connection, love, and intimacy—just like everyone else. The difference lies in how they navigate and express these feelings.

Avoidants often crave relationships but struggle to balance their need for closeness and their fear of vulnerability. They may feel swamped by emotional intimacy or worry about losing their independence. This internal tension can lead to contradictory behaviors, like pulling away as a relationship becomes serious or hesitating to express affection. But it's not a lack of desire for connection—it's the fear of what that connection might cost.

- Avoidant People Only Care About Themselves

Another common misconception is that avoidants are selfish or self-absorbed, caring only about their own needs and neglecting their partners. While it's true that avoidants tend to prioritize their independence, this behavior is usually a defense mechanism rather than a lack of empathy or concern for others.

Avoidants protect themselves by focusing inward, especially in emotionally draining situations. This can make them seem aloof or indifferent, but beneath the surface, many avoidants care deeply about their partners. They may not always know how to express that care in visible or reassuring ways, but it's there. In fact, avoidants are typically loyal to the few people they allow into their inner circle.

- Avoidant People Never Experience Anxiety in Relationships

There's a misconception that avoidants are immune to the emotional struggles of relationships. After all, they seem calm and composed on the outside, right? But just because avoidants don't show their anxiety outwardly doesn't mean they don't feel it.

For many avoidants, anxiety exists beneath the surface, hidden behind a façade of self-sufficiency. They may feel panicked at the thought of losing their independence or worry about being "trapped" in a relationship. While this anxiety often manifests as a need to pull back or create distance, it's driven by fear rather than apathy.

- Avoidant People Can't Change

Perhaps the most damaging myth about avoidant attachment is the belief that avoidants are incapable of change. While it's true that breaking free from avoidant patterns can be challenging, personal growth and transformation are possible.

Avoidants aren't static beings, stuck forever in their attachment style. They can learn to navigate vulnerability and build deeper connections with self-awareness, supportive environments, and intentional effort. Change doesn't happen overnight, but it's important to remember that avoidant behaviors aren't permanent traits—they're adaptive strategies that can be gradually unlearned over time.

For partners of avoidant individuals, the key is to foster a sense of safety and understanding. Avoidants often need time and patience to take small steps toward vulnerability, and they thrive in relationships where their boundaries are respected. With the proper support, avoidants can move toward what psychologists call "earned security," finding a balance between independence and intimacy.

48

- Dismissive Avoidants Don't Care About Relationships

This is perhaps the most common—and the most harmful—misconception about dismissive avoidants. Their behaviors might seem cold or indifferent from an outsider's perspective, leading those around them to mistakenly assume they don't care. But in reality, avoidants care deeply about their relationships. Their distance often stems from a fear of being hurt or being overwhelmed, not from a lack of affection or interest.

Dismissive avoidants may not express their emotions in traditional ways, but that doesn't mean they don't feel them. They may struggle to articulate their feelings or show affection, but their care often shows up in other forms, like loyalty, practical support, or simply being present. Recognizing these less apparent forms of love can help partners better understand their avoidant loved ones.

- Avoidants Are Selfish and Don't Consider Their Partner's Feelings

It's easy to mistake avoidant behaviors for selfishness, but the reality is far more nuanced. Avoidants often struggle with empathy—not because they don't care, but because they're focused on managing their emotions and maintaining their independence. In survival mode, protecting themselves can take precedence over considering others' feelings.

However, this doesn't mean avoidants are incapable of empathy. When given the tools and space to process their emotions, they can develop a greater awareness of their partner's needs and learn to engage in relationships with more thoughtfulness.

Misconceptions about avoidant attachment can create unnecessary tension and misunderstanding in relationships. By reframing these beliefs, we can approach avoidant individuals with greater compassion and recognize their behaviors for what they are: protective mechanisms, not flaws.

Understanding these behaviors is the first step toward growth and connection if you or someone you love has an avoidant attachment style. Avoidants are not "cold" or "selfish"—they're human beings navigating complex emotional patterns. With patience, support, and mutual effort, avoidant individuals and their partners can build thriving relationships, even in the face of attachment challenges.

DISMISSIVE VS FEARFUL AVOIDANT

Insecure attachment styles can be divided into two categories: Anxious and Avoidant. Each has its behaviors and patterns of behavior in relationships, but while anxiety has only one attachment style, the avoidant attachment style is further broken down into two subs:

- Dismissive avoidant
- Fearful avoidant

Understanding the difference between dismissive-avoidant and fearful-avoidant is essential for fostering healthier relationships and emotional well-being. Although both attachment styles share a common thread of avoiding intimacy and trust, they differ significantly in their motivations, behaviors, and coping mechanisms. By exploring these distinctions, we can better navigate relationships and support ourselves and our partners.

FEARFUL AVOIDANT ATTACHMENT: THE PUSH-PULL OF CONNECTION

The fearful-avoidant attachment style, also referred to as disorganized attachment, is typically rooted in inconsistent or traumatic experiences with caregivers. These early experiences create a conflicting dynamic: the desire for intimacy coexists with a fear of getting hurt. As a result, individuals with this attachment style often send mixed signals, shifting between pursuing closeness and retreating from it.

Characteristics of Fearful Avoidant Attachment

- Ambivalence Toward Relationships: Fearful avoidants want deep connections but are simultaneously terrified of vulnerability. This leads to a push-pull dynamic in which they alternate between chasing intimacy and withdrawing to protect themselves.
- Emotional Turmoil: Intense emotions are a hallmark of this attachment style. Fearful

avoidants often experience rapid shifts between anxiety, anger, and despair, creating confusion for themselves and their partners.

- Trust Issues: Past trauma and inconsistent caregiving leave fearful avoidants doubting others' intentions. They may frequently question their partner's loyalty or motives, which can lead to misunderstandings and conflicts.

- Self-Sabotage: To avoid potential rejection or pain, fearful avoidants may engage in behaviors that undermine their relationships, such as dodging commitment or stirring up unnecessary conflict.

- Insecurity: Fearful avoidants struggle with low self-worth, believing they are unlovable or incapable of maintaining a healthy, stable relationship.

DISMISSIVE AVOIDANT ATTACHMENT: THE ARMOR OF INDEPENDENCE

On the other hand, the dismissive-avoidant attachment is characterized by a strong preference for independence and emotional self-reliance. Unlike fearful avoidants, dismissive avoidants are less likely to feel conflicted about their avoidance—they actively prioritize autonomy and distance themselves from emotional intimacy. This attachment style usually develops in childhood environments where emotional expression was discouraged or caregivers were emotionally unavailable.

Characteristics of Dismissive Avoidant Attachment

- Emotional Detachment: Dismissive avoidants are often perceived as emotionally distant or aloof. They suppress their feelings and may struggle to connect with the emotions of others, leading to disconnection in relationships.
- High Need for Independence: They see themselves as self-reliant and may resist relying on others or allowing others to depend on them. Relationships are often seen as potential threats to their autonomy.
- Avoidance of Vulnerability: Dismissive avoidants tend to avoid situations requiring emotional closeness, preferring superficial relationships or casual interactions.

54

- Devaluation of Relationships: They may downplay the importance of relationships, focusing instead on work, hobbies, or other interests. This devaluation can make partners feel unimportant or neglected.
- Difficulty Responding to Others' Needs: Dismissive avoidants may struggle to empathize with their partner's feelings or needs, often seeming indifferent or uncaring.

KEY DIFFERENCES BETWEEN FEARFUL AND DISMISSIVE AVOIDANT ATTACHMENT

Motivation for Avoidance

- Fearful Avoidant: Driven by a *fear of rejection* and a conflicted desire for connection.
- Dismissive Avoidant: Driven by a *need for independence* and a belief in self-reliance.

Desire for Intimacy

- Fearful Avoidant: Craves closeness but fears it, creating an internal conflict that often results in erratic behaviors.

- Dismissive Avoidant: Actively avoids intimacy, viewing it as a threat to their autonomy.

Emotional Expression

- Fearful Avoidant: Experiences emotions intensely but struggles to regulate or express them, leading to emotional volatility.
- Dismissive Avoidant: Minimizes or downplays emotions to maintain detachment, resulting in communication breakdowns.

Trust Issues

- Fearful Avoidant: Trust issues stem from past trauma or inconsistent caregiving, leading to a fear of betrayal or abandonment.
- Dismissive Avoidant: Trust issues arise from the belief that others are unreliable, reinforcing their reliance on self-sufficiency.

Approach to Relationships

- Fearful Avoidant: Alternates between seeking closeness and withdrawing, creating a push-pull dynamic that can confuse their partners.

- Dismissive Avoidant: Maintains distance and prefers relationships that require minimal emotional involvement.

Impact on Partners

- Fearful Avoidant: Partners may feel frustrated by their unpredictability, emotional outbursts, or mixed signals.
- Dismissive Avoidant: Partners may feel neglected, unimportant, or unloved due to the avoidant's emotional detachment and lack of engagement.

Understanding the distinctions between dismissive and fearful avoidant attachment is crucial for navigating relationships. While both attachment styles involve avoidance, their underlying motivations and expressions differ significantly. Recognizing these differences allows for greater empathy and tailored strategies for growth and connection.

For example:

- If you're in a relationship with a fearful avoidant, focusing on building trust and creating a sense of safety can help them feel more secure in the relationship.
- With a dismissive avoidant, it's essential to respect their need for independence while encouraging gradual steps toward vulnerability and emotional expression.

For both attachment styles, therapy can be a transformative tool.

- Fearful Avoidant Therapy Goals: Focuses on building self-worth, regulating emotions, and rebuilding trust in others.
- Dismissive Avoidant Therapy Goals: Aims to reconnect with suppressed emotions, embrace vulnerability, and foster deeper connections.

Regardless of attachment style, therapy provides a safe space to explore fears, develop healthier emotional responses, and work toward a secure attachment style.

Although dismissive and fearful avoidants share similar challenges with intimacy, their differences lie in how they approach and cope with relationships. Understanding these distinctions can help navigate relationships with greater empathy and clarity, whether we're working on our attachment style or supporting a loved one with theirs. With time and effort, growth is possible for both styles and meaningful connections can flourish.

CASE STUDY: EMMA AND DAVID

I first met Emma at the start of their relationship, a stark contrast to her previous dating experiences. While Emma enjoyed flirting and attention, she always maintained emotional distance. David, however, was different—he entered the relationship seeking a serious, long-term connection.

David had a history of serious relationships and entered their dynamic with the expectation of a long-term commitment. Emma, however, initially viewed their connection as a casual summer fling. Three years later, they were married—a testament to the complexities of their journey.

When David said, "I love you," within six months of dating, Emma froze. She didn't reciprocate until nearly a year later. For someone with avoidant tendencies, expressing love is like a leap into the unknown—one fraught with vulnerability and risk. Even as she grew closer to David, Emma clung to her independence. She frequently told friends, "If this doesn't work out, I'll just be the rich, cool aunt who travels the world," and she meant it. She genuinely believed she'd be fine without him.

This mindset is a hallmark of avoidant attachment: the constant reassurance that leaving is always an option. Even after realizing she wanted a future with David, Emma's avoidant tendencies continued to emerge.

Emma and David dated for two years before getting engaged, and the road to that engagement wasn't smooth. Whenever a problem arose, Emma's instinct was to avoid it entirely. Instead of talking through issues, she'd go to the gym or distract herself with other activities. For her, emotions were messy, and addressing them felt pointless. In contrast, David wanted to resolve their conflicts and connect emotionally, but it took Emma years to learn how to communicate with him in a way that would strengthen their bond.

Even after they married, Emma's inner dialogue remained shaped by avoidance. When arguments happened, she would think, We don't have kids yet. I can still leave without all the drama. These escape routes weren't a reflection of her love for David but rather a manifestation of her deep discomfort with vulnerability. She confessed, "I hate thinking this way because I don't want to leave. I love him. But I don't know how to stop these thoughts when things get tough."

Let's break down Emma's behaviors and patterns and connect them to the core characteristics of avoidant attachment. As you read through these, reflect on whether any of them resonate with your own experiences:

1. **Escape Routes in Relationships:** Emma constantly entertained the thought of leaving her relationship whenever conflict arose. This mental "exit strategy" is a hallmark of avoidant attachment. For avoidants, having an escape

plan provides a sense of security against potential emotional pain. Even though she doesn't have a real desire to end the relationship, she'll create distance to detach herself from David, believing this will shield her from further hurt.

Reflection: Do you often find yourself thinking about how you'd leave a relationship, even when you care deeply for your partner? Do you feel comforted by the thought that you could walk away at any time? This behavior reflects a deep-seated fear of being trapped or losing control within the relationship.

2. **Struggles with Emotional Closeness:** Emma took a long time to say "I love you" to David. She had difficulty opening up emotionally and connecting on a deeper level. Avoidants often fear vulnerability because it feels like giving up control.

Reflection: Do you hesitate to express your feelings, even when you feel them strongly? Does saying "I love you" or showing affection make you feel exposed or uneasy? This reluctance to express affection is a common manifestation of emotional guarding.

3. **Avoidance of Emotions:** Emma avoided dealing with her emotions by focusing on external activities like going to the gym. Avoidants often suppress their feelings, choosing to ignore or dismiss them rather than face the discomfort of emotional pain.

   Reflection: Do you tend to push your emotions aside when things get tough? Do you distract yourself with work, hobbies, or other activities instead of addressing your feelings? This avoidance of emotions is a key deactivation strategy.

4. **Hyper-Independent Mindset:** Emma envisioned herself thriving on her own, convincing herself she didn't need David or anyone else to be happy. Avoidants often take pride in their independence, viewing reliance on others as a weakness.

Reflection: Do you prefer to handle everything independently, even when help is available? Do you see dependence on others as something to avoid? This hyper-independence is a core characteristic of the avoidant attachment style.

5. **Emotional Detachment During Conflict:** During fights, Emma's instinct was to withdraw rather than engage. Avoidants often struggle to remain present during conflict, choosing to shut down or create distance to protect themselves.

Reflection: When conflict arises, do you find yourself pulling away emotionally? Do you avoid discussing problems because it feels too overwhelming or pointless? This emotional detachment during conflict is another common deactivation strategy.

What We Can Learn from Emma

Emma's story vividly illustrates the core struggles of avoidant attachment: the fear of closeness, the constant need for independence, and the tendency to

64

avoid emotions and conflict. These patterns, while intended to protect, ultimately create barriers to genuine connection. If you can relate to Emma's experiences, remember that awareness is the first step toward change. Avoidant attachment is not a fixed trait but a learned pattern that can be changed with self-compassion and intentional effort.

Reflect on the characteristics you see in Emma and consider how they might be impacting your relationships. What small steps can you take toward greater vulnerability and connection?

Recap: This chapter covered the origins of avoidant attachment, tracing its roots to early childhood experiences and examining how it manifests in adulthood through behaviors like emotional withdrawal and hyper-independence. You've learned that avoidant attachment is a learned protective response, not a personal flaw. In the next chapter, we'll delve deeper into how these patterns can sabotage connections and offer practical strategies for building secure and fulfilling relationships.

CHAPTER 2: BREAKING DOWN THE WALLS

"The walls we build around us to keep others out are not made of stone but fear." – Unknown

Have you ever found yourself keeping someone at arm's length, even when you longed to let them in? Perhaps you've sabotaged a promising relationship, avoided difficult conversations, or dismissed emotional closeness as "too much." It's not that you don't care; it's the intense wave of emotions that true vulnerability evokes. This is the central paradox of avoidant attachment: the desire for connection clashing with an instinctive need for distance.

This chapter explores the subtle ways avoidant behaviors hinder meaningful relationships. By identifying these patterns and understanding their roots, you can begin to dismantle the walls you've built and make space for authentic connection.

How You Unknowingly Sabotage Connections

Avoidant attachment often operates beneath conscious awareness. The avoidance can feel so natural that you may not even realize how your behaviors are impacting your relationships. However, taking the time to reflect can reveal patterns that get in the way of the intimacy you seek.

- **Avoiding Emotional Depth:** Avoidants often sabotage deep emotional connections by keeping relationships surface-level and detached. Instead of engaging in meaningful, vulnerable conversations, they may unconsciously redirect discussions to neutral or practical topics—work, schedules, hobbies, or even using humor as a shield. For example, if a partner expresses feeling lonely or needing reassurance, an avoidant might respond with a joke or downplay their partner's emotions rather than engaging with the depth of the conversation. This pattern creates emotional distance, leaving their loved ones feeling unseen, unheard, and emotionally disconnected—as though they are in a relationship with someone physically present but emotionally absent.

- **Deflecting During Conflict:** Conflict is inevitable in any relationship, but for avoidants, it feels threatening. You might avoid difficult conversations, dismiss your partner's concerns, or change the subject when emotions run high. While this provides temporary relief, it leads to unresolved issues and lingering tension.

- **Magnifying Flaws:** When relationships feel too close, avoidants may unconsciously focus on their partner's imperfections, using these perceived flaws to justify emotional distance. You might think, *They're too needy,* or *They don't really get me*, even if these thoughts aren't entirely accurate.

- **Keeping an Escape Route:** The idea of being able to leave a relationship at any time can be comforting for avoidants. This mental "exit strategy" provides a sense of control but prevents the ability to fully engage and invest in the relationship.

EXPLORING EMOTIONAL TRIGGERS

Understanding what triggers avoidant behaviors is crucial for breaking down these walls. These triggers typically arise when emotional closeness feels threatening, activating defense mechanisms. These triggers aren't always obvious and can vary from person to person, though some common themes emerge.

Common Triggers for Avoidants:

- **Requests for Emotional Vulnerability:** Being asked to open up, share feelings, or show affection can be challenging. This isn't because avoidants lack feelings but because expressing them makes them feel exposed and vulnerable to potential judgment or rejection. The request can feel like a demand, triggering a sense of pressure and a desire to pull away.
    - *Examples:* Being asked, "How are you *really* feeling?" or being told, "I need you to

be more open with me." Additionally, you might be on the receiving end of a heartfelt declaration of love before feeling ready.

- **Perceived Criticism:** Avoidants are highly sensitive to criticism, even when it's constructive feedback. This sensitivity stems from a deep-seated fear of inadequacy and a tendency to interpret neutral or even positive feedback as negative. A partner pointing out a mistake, even gently, can trigger feelings of shame, defensiveness, and a desire to withdraw to protect their self-esteem.

  - *Examples:* A partner suggesting, "Maybe we could try communicating differently," or hearing a casual remark like, "You seem a little quiet today."

- **Future Commitments:** Discussions about marriage, children, moving in together, or even making long-term plans can feel suffocating for avoidants. These conversations signify a loss of independence and a perceived 'trap" of commitment. The thought of being tied down can provoke anxiety and a strong urge to escape the situation, either mentally or physically.

- ○ *Examples:* A partner saying, "I can't wait to spend the rest of my life with you," discussing buying a house together, or planning a vacation more than a few months in advance.
- **Emotional Intensity (in Others):** Whether it's a partner expressing strong emotions (sadness, anger, joy) or a friend seeking comfort during a difficult time, emotionally charged situations can be extremely challenging for avoidants. They may feel ill-equipped to handle the intensity of others' emotions, fearing they will be responsible for "fixing" the situation. This can lead to discomfort, withdrawal, or attempts to minimize or dismiss the other person's feelings.
  - ○ *Examples:* A partner crying after a loss, a friend expressing intense anger about a situation, or even a partner expressing joy and excitement.
- **Expressions of Neediness or Dependence (in Others):** Being on the receiving end of what avoidants perceive as neediness or dependence can be a significant trigger. It can activate fears of being controlled or engulfed by another person's

emotions. They may interpret these expressions as demands on their time, energy, and emotional resources, leading them to distance themselves.

- *Examples:* A partner frequently asking for reassurance, constantly seeking attention, or expressing a strong fear of being alone.

- **Feeling "Smothered" or "Controlled":** An avoidant may react defensively if they feel like their autonomy is threatened. This includes seemingly innocent behaviors like a partner wanting to spend a lot of time together or offering unsolicited advice.

  - *Examples:* A partner wanting to spend every weekend together, offering advice about their career or hobbies, or even a partner frequently checking in throughout the day.

Why These Situations Are Triggering:

These triggers all share a common thread: they represent a perceived threat to the avoidant's independence and sense of control. They tap into deep-seated fears of vulnerability, helplessness, and loss of autonomy. Understanding this underlying fear is key to understanding why these seemingly ordinary situations can be distressing for avoidants.

How Triggers Manifest:

When triggered, avoidants may engage in various deactivation strategies, such as:

- **Emotional Withdrawal:** Becoming distant, unresponsive, or shutting down emotionally.
- **Physical Withdrawal:** Leaving the situation, finding excuses to be alone, or creating physical distance.
- **Minimizing or Dismissing Emotions:** Downplaying feelings or changing the subject.
- **Focusing on Flaws:** Magnifying their partner's imperfections to rationalize creating distance.
- **Creating Conflict:** Picking fights or starting arguments to create distance and justify withdrawing.

Recognizing these triggers and understanding how they manifest allows avoidants to develop healthier coping mechanisms and work toward building more secure connections.

Emotional Numbing and Repression

Repression, a psychological defense mechanism introduced by Sigmund Freud, involves unconsciously blocking distressing thoughts, memories, and feelings from conscious awareness. Repression operates beneath the surface, unlike suppression (a conscious effort to ignore emotions). While it provides temporary protection from emotional pain, it has long-term consequences, including emotional numbness, which impedes genuine connection and emotional well-being. Research suggests that up to 30% of adults struggle with emotional avoidance or repression as a coping mechanism, often leading to difficulties in relationships and mental health challenges. (Kring & Sloan, 2009)

Signs and Symptoms of Repression:

- **Emotional Numbness:** Difficulty identifying or expressing feelings, often described as feeling "numb" or disconnected.
- **Mood Swings:** Unexpected shifts in mood, such as moving from happiness to irritability without an apparent cause.

- **Avoidance Behaviors:** Avoiding specific topics, people, or situations that might trigger buried emotions.
- **Compulsive Behaviors or Addictions:** Overreliance on distractions like excessive work, shopping, or substance use.
- **Physical Symptoms:** Unexplained physical symptoms like headaches, muscle tension, or digestive issues.

THE CONSEQUENCES OF EMOTIONAL NUMBNESS

While emotional numbness can provide temporary relief from emotional pain, it can take a significant toll over time. Living in a state of emotional detachment deprives individuals from experiencing the full spectrum of human emotions, including joy, love, and connection.

Impact on Relationships

Emotional numbness creates barriers in relationships, as individuals may struggle to connect with others on a deep emotional level. Partners, friends, and family members may feel shut out, leading to frustration, miscommunication, and strain in the relationship.

Studies show that 67% of individuals in relationships with emotionally repressed partners report feeling emotionally neglected, leading to higher rates of breakups and divorce. (The Journal of Social and Personal Relationships, 2019)

Mental Health Challenges

Repressed emotions don't disappear; they often resurface in unexpected ways, contributing to mental health issues such as depression, anxiety, and even post-traumatic stress disorder (PTSD). The inability to process and release emotions leaves unresolved pain that impacts overall well-being. A 2020 study published in Frontiers in Psychology found that emotion suppression is significantly linked to increased stress levels and a 40% higher risk of developing anxiety or depression.

Loss of Identity

Without access to their complete range of emotions, individuals may experience a sense of disconnection from themselves. Emotional repression can lead to an identity crisis, where a person struggles to understand who they are or what they truly value.

Physical Health Problems

Emotional numbness doesn't just affect the mind—it takes a toll on the body as well. Chronic stress from repressed emotions can manifest in fatigue, sleep disturbances, and even long-term conditions like cardiovascular issues or autoimmune disorders.

People who repress emotions are twice as likely to experience chronic pain conditions, such as migraines, irritable bowel syndrome (IBS), and fibromyalgia. (American Psychosomatic Society, 2018)

HOW REPRESSION SHAPES AVOIDANT ATTACHMENT

For avoidantly attached individuals, repression often becomes a default coping mechanism. They unconsciously brush aside difficult emotions, relying on independence and self-sufficiency. While this emotional detachment may feel like a safe haven, it prevents full engagement in relationships and addressing the root of their fears. Repression becomes a survival strategy, leading to emotional numbness and distance from loved ones.

THE LONG-TERM IMPACT OF REPRESSION ON AVOIDANTS

- **Relationship Strain:** Difficulty connecting emotionally that results in feelings of neglect and disconnection.
- **Missed Opportunities for Growth:** Preventing the addressing of root causes of fears, hindering personal and relational growth.
- **Increased Loneliness:** Creating a sense of isolation and emptiness despite independence.
- **Health Implications:** Contributing to chronic stress and long-term health problems.

Emotional repression and numbness may feel like protective shields, but they come with major downsides. Comprehending the origin of repression and its impact will allow you to take the first steps toward reconnecting with your emotions and building fulfilling relationships.

RECOGNIZING THE FEAR OF DEPENDENCE

Avoidants often pride themselves on self-reliance and independence, which can mask a deeper fear of dependence. Relying on someone else can feel like losing control.

Signs of the Fear of Dependence:

- Avoiding asking for help, even when needed.
- Feeling uncomfortable when someone depends on you for emotional support.
- Viewing emotional closeness as a threat to autonomy.
- Equating vulnerability with weakness.

This fear often leads to emotional distancing despite a desire for connection.

CASE STUDY: MICHAEL AND SARAH

Michael is a successful entrepreneur who prides himself on his independence. He's charismatic but has a history of short-lived relationships.

When Michael began dating Sarah, he was initially drawn to her emotional openness but as the relationship progressed, he began to feel trapped. He zeroed in on Sarah's so-called flaws—her desperate need for reassurance, her unpredictable mood swings—convincing himself they were incompatible.

Michael would change the subject whenever Sarah wanted to discuss their future or withdraw. Eventually, Sarah confronted him about his distance. Instead of addressing the issue, Michael ended the relationship, rationalizing that being alone was preferable to "drama."

Michael's story exemplifies how fear of emotional closeness and dependence can lead to prioritizing self-protection over connection, leaving both parties unfulfilled.

RECOGNIZING AND ADDRESSING YOUR PATTERNS

Self-Reflection Questions:

- Do I avoid difficult conversations because of discomfort?
- What is my instinctive reaction when feeling overwhelmed in a relationship?
- Do I tend to focus on my partner's flaws rather than their strengths?
- Do I often feel the need to maintain an "escape route" in relationships?

Small Steps Toward Change:

Avoidant attachment often involves suppressing or minimizing emotions to maintain a sense of control and avoid discomfort. However, acknowledging and understanding your emotional landscape is crucial for breaking free from these patterns. Here's how:

- **Practice Emotional Awareness:**
  - **Acknowledge Your Feelings:** Begin by simply noticing your emotions. Don't judge them or try to suppress them.

- **Example:** Instead of dismissing feelings of sadness as "weakness," acknowledge them: "I'm feeling sad today. I wonder why."
  - **Label Your Emotions:** Put words to your feelings. Are you feeling anxious, overwhelmed, lonely, or frustrated?
    - **Example:** Instead of just feeling "off," try to identify the specific emotion: "I'm feeling anxious about the upcoming presentation."
  - **Journaling as a Tool:** Regularly journaling can help you track your emotions, identify patterns, and gain a deeper understanding of your emotional landscape.
    - **Example:** Write about a recent interaction that triggered feelings of discomfort. What emotions did you experience? How did you react?
- **Engage in Difficult Conversations:**
  - **Challenge Yourself to Stay Present:** When faced with conflict or disagreement,

actively resist the urge to withdraw or shut down.

- **Example:** Instead of changing the subject or walking away, take a deep breath and remind yourself that open communication is important.

o **Focus on Active Listening:** Truly listen to your partner's perspective, even if you disagree. Reflect back what you've heard to ensure you understand their viewpoint.

- **Example:** Instead of interrupting, try to summarize your partner's feelings: "It sounds like you're feeling hurt and disappointed."

o **Express Yourself Calmly and Assertively:** Use "I" statements to express your own feelings and needs without blaming or accusing.

- **Example:** Instead of saying, "You always...", try: "I feel hurt when..." or "I need..."

- **Reframe Vulnerability as a Strength:**

- o **Challenge the Narrative:** Reframe vulnerability as a sign of courage and trust, not weakness.
  - ▪ **Example:** Instead of seeing vulnerability as a threat, view it as an opportunity to deepen connection.
- o **Practice Small Acts of Vulnerability:** Start with small, manageable steps, such as sharing a personal anecdote or expressing a concern to a trusted friend.
- o **Observe the Positive Outcomes:** Notice how vulnerability can lead to deeper connection and understanding in your relationships.

By consistently practicing these strategies, you can begin to break down the walls of avoidance and cultivate a more open and connected way of being.

Recap: This chapter discussed avoidant behaviors in relationships, including emotional numbing and repression—defense mechanisms used to suppress feelings and avoid discomfort. We examined how these patterns lead to self-sabotage and the triggers that

85

perpetuate cycles of withdrawal. In the next chapter, we'll analyze the emotional avoidance cycle and strategies for building resilience in the face of discomfort.

Key Points to Remember:

- Emotional numbing and repression can create a false sense of control but often lead to disconnection and loneliness.
- Avoidance behaviors are often triggered by fears of dependence or emotional vulnerability.
- Awareness of these triggers and patterns is the first step toward breaking free from them.

Consider the triggers and behaviors you identified in this chapter. How might they be holding you back from a deeper connection? What incremental steps can you take to begin breaking the cycle?

CHAPTER 3: FROM AVOIDANCE TO AWARENESS

"You can't heal what you don't allow yourself to feel."
— Unknown

Have you ever sensed a persistent distance in your relationships, even when everything seems fine on the surface? Perhaps you instinctively withdraw when emotions run deep, as though you're opening a door to a room you've kept locked for years. You genuinely care about your partner, and you know they care about you, but there's a lingering distance that you can't quite explain. Whenever emotions start to intensify, you instinctively retreat. You might change the subject, avoid the conversation, or shut down altogether.

This chapter is about finding the courage to open that door—not all at once, but one small step at a time. By understanding the emotional avoidance cycle and developing self-awareness, you can break free from the patterns that disconnect you from yourself and your relationships.

THE EMOTIONAL AVOIDANCE CYCLE

Avoidance doesn't happen by accident. It's a learned response that often originates in childhood. This behavior becomes a cycle of self-protection, typically following this pattern:

1. Trigger: Something happens that stirs uncomfortable emotions, such as criticism, a partner asking for reassurance, or a moment of vulnerability.
2. Emotional Response: You may feel overwhelmed, anxious, or unsure of how to handle the situation.

3. Avoidant Behavior: To manage the discomfort, you engage in avoidant behaviors, such as withdrawing, deflecting, or minimizing the importance of the situation.

4. Short-Term Relief: Avoidance provides temporary relief, making you feel more in control and less vulnerable.

5. Long-Term Impact: The unresolved emotions don't go away—they linger beneath the surface, creating distance in your relationships and reinforcing the avoidance cycle.

To illustrate how the Emotional Avoidance Cycle plays out in relationships, let's look at one of my clients, Ben—a driven and successful marketing executive who often felt uneasy in his relationship with his partner, Caron.

Caron, a sensitive and emotionally attuned individual, valued quality time and emotional connection. She occasionally expressed concerns about Ben's long work hours and how they impacted their relationship.

The Trigger

One evening, Caron gently brought up her feelings, saying, "I miss spending time with you. I know work has been busy, but I'd love for us to set aside some time together."

Emotional Response

Ben immediately felt a wave of discomfort. Conversations like this always made him feel pressured and defensive. Deep down, he worried that Caron was being too needy or that she was asking for more than he could give. At the same time, a part of him felt guilty—he knew he had been distant, but acknowledging that would mean confronting his own emotional discomfort.

Avoidant Behavior

Instead of engaging with Caron's feelings, Ben deflected. He quickly changed the subject, saying, "I know, work has been insane lately. It's just this project—I'll have more time after next week." He downplayed her concerns, minimizing the issue with a casual, "Don't worry, we'll figure it out soon."

Short-Term Relief

In the moment, this strategy worked for Ben. He didn't have to confront his emotions or engage in an uncomfortable conversation. He felt a brief sense of control, as though he had successfully avoided conflict and preserved his independence.

Long-Term Impact

But while Ben felt relief, Caron felt dismissed and unheard. Over time, she began to withdraw emotionally, sensing that her needs weren't important to Ben. She started hesitating to share her feelings, fearing she would be brushed aside again.

Meanwhile, Ben misinterpreted Caron's withdrawal as emotional distance or disapproval, reinforcing his belief that intimacy leads to pressure or judgment. He became even more avoidant, further widening the emotional gap between them.

THE SELF-PERPETUATING CYCLE

This pattern continued, subtly eroding the foundation of their relationship. Ben's avoidance, while providing temporary relief, led to:

- Increased emotional distance between him and Caron.
- Growing resentment from Caron, who felt unappreciated and unheard.
- A deeper sense of isolation for Ben, reinforcing his belief that emotional conversations are risky or unnecessary.

This example highlights how the Emotional Avoidance Cycle operates in real relationships. By understanding this pattern, individuals can identify their own avoidance behaviors and take steps to break free from the cycle—choosing connection over avoidance, growth over stagnation, and openness over fear.

BREAKING THE CYCLE

Breaking the cycle of avoidant attachment is challenging but entirely possible. Our brains possess neuroplasticity—the ability to change and form new neural pathways—meaning we can rewire ingrained patterns and develop healthier ways of relating. These childhood survival patterns can be transformed with consistent practice and intention. Here are some key practices to help you move toward a more secure attachment style:

- **Building Vulnerability and Connection:**
  - Take calculated risks by sharing your feelings with your partner, even when uncomfortable.
  - Gradually share your needs in small, manageable ways, increasing openness over time.
  - Practice active listening and validate your partner's needs.
  - Shift your mindset from "I" to "we," considering the needs of the partnership.
  - Practice empathy instead of reacting defensively during conflict.
- **Increasing Self-Awareness and Seeking Support:**

- o Pay attention to your partner's emotions and needs, expanding your awareness beyond your internal thoughts. Try small but intentional actions, such as asking, "How was your day?" and genuinely listening without rushing to change the subject.

- o Learn to ask for and graciously accept help. Practice allowing small moments of support from others—whether it's accepting a favor, sharing a personal struggle, or asking for reassurance. Remember, receiving support doesn't mean losing control; it strengthens trust and deepens relationships.

- **Using Resources to Guide Your Growth**

  - o Books and professional guidance can be powerful tools for self-discovery and healing. Consider exploring resources that align with your journey toward secure attachment and emotional well-being.

  - o Recommended Reads by Richard Banks:

    - *The Path to Secure Attachment* – A practical guide to understanding attachment styles and rewiring your relationship patterns for greater emotional security.

- *Anxious Attachment and Avoidant Detachment* – A deep dive into the push-pull dynamic between anxious and avoidant partners, offering insights and strategies to foster healthier relationships.

- *How to Deal with Stress, Depression, and Anxiety* – Essential tools to manage emotional distress, reframe negative thought patterns, and cultivate mental resilience.

- **Seeking Professional Support**

  o Therapy—especially with an attachment-focused professional—can provide personalized strategies to help you navigate emotional challenges and build a more secure attachment style.

  o Online courses, support groups, or relationship coaching can also offer structured guidance to help you recognize patterns and implement change.

Healing begins with intention. With time, these practices can help you reframe your relationship with vulnerability and connection.

RECOGNIZING AND NAMING EMOTIONS

Emotions are integral to the human experience. They shape our reactions, influence our decisions, and impact our overall well-being. Recognizing emotions can feel like an insurmountable challenge for many people, particularly those with avoidant attachments. Years of emotional suppression or trauma can make feelings unclear, inaccessible, or burdensome.

For some of my clients, even identifying what they are feeling is a struggle, let alone managing or expressing those emotions. This is particularly true for individuals who have experienced chronic stress or trauma. In these cases, emotional numbness becomes a survival mechanism—a way to cope with the pain of vulnerability. While this may have served a protective purpose in the past, it also creates barriers to authentic connection and emotional health in the present.

Why Naming Emotions Matters

Recognizing and naming emotions is the foundation of emotional awareness and regulation. Emotions are signals, much like a dashboard light in a car, alerting us to what's happening internally. When we fail to identify these signals, we risk ignoring important needs or reacting impulsively in ways that harm ourselves or others.

Naming emotions allows us to:

1. Disengage from their intensity by creating a space for observation
2. Interrupt cycles of rumination by shifting from vague distress to concrete understanding
3. Re-engage adaptively by responding thoughtfully rather than reacting impulsively

Practical Steps for Recognizing Emotions

1. Start with Psychoeducation: Learn about the nature of emotions. Understanding that

emotions are natural and temporary helps normalize your experience and reduces fear of feeling them.

2. Pause and Reflect: When you feel discomfort, pause and ask yourself: What am I feeling right now? Where in my body do I feel it?

3. Use Tools Like an Emotion Wheel: Emotion wheels help expand your emotional vocabulary, moving beyond basic descriptors like "happy" or "sad" to more nuanced terms like "hopeful," "irritated," or "overwhelmed."

4. Mindfulness and Presence: Practice mindfulness to tune into your emotional state without judgment. Pay attention to your feelings as they arise and allow them to exist without trying to suppress or fix them.

5. Journal Your Emotions: Regularly writing down your feelings and the events that triggered them can help you identify patterns over time. Journaling is a powerful tool for building self-awareness.

Reflection Exercise

Take a moment to reflect on a recent situation when you felt emotional discomfort. Instead of just reviewing what happened, let's distinguish between constructive and avoidant responses to gain deeper self-awareness and recognize patterns that may be holding you back.

Step 1: Identify the Emotion

- What emotion were you feeling in that moment?
- Did you acknowledge it, or did you push it aside?

Step 2: Identify the Trigger

- What situation, conversation, or thought sparked this emotion?
- Was it an external event (a comment, action, or conflict) or something internal (a memory, assumption, or fear)?

Step 3: Examine Your Response

- How did you react in that moment? Did you withdraw, dismiss the emotion, deflect the conversation, or change the subject?
- Did you feel the need to create distance, avoid discussing the issue, or downplay what you were experiencing?

Step 4: Was Your Response Constructive or Avoidant?

Avoidant Responses (Self-Protection Mode)

- **Emotional suppression:** Pushing emotions aside or convincing yourself it's "not a big deal."
- **Deflection:** Using humor, sarcasm, or logic to avoid engaging with feelings.
- **Withdrawal:** Physically or emotionally distancing yourself, shutting down, or distracting yourself with work, social media, or other tasks.
- **Minimization:** Dismissing emotions as irrational, overreacting, or unnecessary.

- **Control-seeking:** Avoiding vulnerability by focusing on facts, solutions, or tasks rather than addressing feelings.

Constructive Responses (Growth-Oriented Mode)

- **Acknowledging the emotion:** Naming what you're feeling without judgment.
- **Self-reflection:** Exploring why this trigger affected you and whether it's tied to past experiences.
- **Engaging instead of withdrawing:** Expressing your feelings rather than shutting down or deflecting.
- **Communicating with openness:** If this situation involved another person, did you share your feelings in a calm, clear way?
- **Seeking support:** Instead of handling everything alone, did you allow yourself to reach out for reassurance or guidance?

Step 5: What Would You Do Differently?

If your response was avoidant, what small change could you make next time to lean into emotional engagement rather than retreat from it?

- Could you take a deep breath and name your feelings before reacting?
- Could you express your discomfort to someone you trust instead of withdrawing?
- Could you sit with the emotion for a moment instead of distracting yourself?

Next time you feel emotional discomfort, challenge yourself to pause and choose a constructive response over an avoidant one. Progress is about making one small change at a time.

TECHNIQUES FOR EMOTIONAL REGULATION

Emotional regulation refers to the ability to influence which emotions you feel, when you experience them, and how you express or handle them. It's a crucial skill for navigating life's challenges without becoming overwhelmed or acting impulsively. When you have healthy emotional regulation, you build resilience, improve your mental health, and achieve social success, while difficulties with regulation can lead to stress, relationship strain, and even physical health issues (Iwakabe et al., 2023).

The good news? Emotional regulation is a skill you can learn and strengthen over time. By using structured practices and strategies, you can expand your emotional bandwidth and respond more effectively to difficult situations.

Core Practices for Emotional Regulation

1. Reframing Negative Thoughts: Instead of catastrophizing, reframe the situation to find a silver lining or learning opportunity. For example, a perceived failure can be seen as a stepping stone for growth.

2. Acceptance and Mindfulness: During moments of intense stress, practice mindfulness and acceptance to calm your nervous system. Acknowledge your emotions without judgment and allow them to pass naturally.

3. Taking Breaks: Recognize when an emotion, such as anger, is escalating. Remove yourself from the situation temporarily to cool down,

ensuring you respond thoughtfully rather than impulsively.

4. Expressing Emotions Constructively: Use calm, assertive communication to express your feelings, rather than bottling them up or lashing out. For instance, saying, "I feel hurt when…" fosters connection and clarity.

5. Problem-Solving: When negative emotions arise, redirect your focus toward identifying actionable steps to address the root cause, reducing the need to overthink.

Evidence-Based Emotional Regulation Techniques

Several research-backed approaches can help improve emotional regulation:

1. Cognitive Reappraisal: Challenge negative thoughts and reframe situations to find alternative perspectives. For instance, rather than seeing criticism as a personal attack, view it as constructive feedback for growth (Buhle et al., 2014).

2. Mindfulness Practice: Cultivate present-moment awareness to observe emotions

without judgment. Consistent mindfulness practice has been shown to improve emotional regulation by increasing emotional awareness and reducing reactivity (Chiesa et al., 2013).

3. **Self-Soothing Techniques:** Engage in activities that calm the nervous system, such as deep breathing, progressive muscle relaxation, or spending time in nature.

4. Acceptance and Commitment Therapy (ACT): ACT encourages you to accept difficult emotions rather than avoid them. By embracing your feelings, you can reduce the distress they cause and focus on actions that align with your values (Blackledge & Hayes, 2001).

5. Dialectical Behavior Therapy (DBT): DBT combines mindfulness with cognitive-behavioral techniques to teach skills like distress tolerance, emotional regulation, and interpersonal effectiveness. Techniques like the TIP skills (temperature change, intense exercise, paced breathing) are particularly effective for calming emotional overwhelm.

Building Your Emotional Regulation Toolkit

Here's how you can start incorporating these techniques into your daily life:

- Daily Emotional Check-Ins: Take a few moments each day to identify how you're feeling and why.
- Practice Mindful Presence: Dedicate 5–10 minutes daily to mindfulness exercises like deep breathing or a body scan to enhance emotional awareness. A body scan helps you notice physical sensations, tension, or discomfort without judgment, reconnecting you to your body and emotions.
- Engage in Constructive Activities: When emotions feel overwhelming, redirect your energy to calming activities like walking, journaling, or listening to music.
- Focus on "We" Thinking: Shift your mindset to consider the needs of your relationships, not just your individual preferences.

For example:

Before: Alex, who has an avoidant attachment style, values independence and prefers to make decisions alone. When his partner, Jamie, suggests planning a weekend getaway together, Alex instinctively feels overwhelmed and responds, "I just need some time to myself this weekend."

After: Instead of reacting automatically, Alex pauses and considers Jamie's perspective. He reminds himself that relationships thrive on mutual effort. Instead of dismissing the idea, he shifts his mindset from "What do I need?" to "What do we need?" He responds, "I really value my alone time, but I also want to spend time with you. How about we plan something for Sunday so we both get what we need?"

Recognizing and regulating emotions is a skill that requires patience, practice, and intention. By understanding the foundations of emotional regulation and incorporating evidence-based strategies into your daily life, you can respond to life's challenges with greater clarity and control. In doing so, you'll strengthen your ability to connect with others, navigate conflict, and embrace vulnerability—a key step toward secure attachment.

CASE STUDY: SALLY AND ALEX

Sally had always been self-sufficient, priding herself on her ability to handle life's challenges alone. However, her avoidance patterns became more apparent when she entered a relationship with Alex.

When Alex shared his anxieties about a work presentation, Sally felt a wave of discomfort. Instead of offering support, she joked, "Well, at least it's not brain surgery!" and changed the subject to weekend plans. This left Alex feeling dismissed and unsupported. When Alex confronted her about her distance, Sarah realized she didn't even know how to identify or express her feelings. She had spent so many years suppressing them that they felt foreign to her.

Determined to break this cycle, Sally began reconnecting with her emotions through journaling, mindfulness, and therapy. She learned to pause when she felt the urge to withdraw and instead ask herself: What am I feeling, and why? Over time, she became more comfortable sitting with her emotions and sharing them with Alex, strengthening their bond.

Moving from avoidance to awareness is a journey of self-discovery and growth. Understanding the emotional avoidance cycle, practicing secure attachment skills, and embracing vulnerability can help rewire your brain for healthier relational patterns. In the following chapter, we'll diver deeper to see how these skills can transform your relationships, helping you navigate connections with greater confidence and ease.

Recap: This chapter focused on emotional awareness and regulation, which are vital for overcoming avoidant tendencies. You learned to identify and name emotions, practice mindfulness, and engage in grounding exercises to manage overwhelming feelings.

We also explored emotional resilience—the ability to face vulnerability and process emotions without retreating. These practices create a strong foundation for cultivating secure attachments and deeper relationships.

CHAPTER 4: NAVIGATING RELATIONSHIPS AS AN AVOIDANT

"Connection is why we're here; it is what gives purpose and meaning to our lives." – Brené Brown

Anthony was the kind of person who seemed to have it all. A successful entrepreneur, he built a thriving business from the ground up, traveled the world for work and pleasure, and prided himself on his independence. Freedom wasn't just a value to him—it was his lifeline. He cherished the ability to make his own decisions, set his own schedule, and live life on his terms. But when it came to relationships, that same freedom felt like a double-edged sword.

At first, every relationship was exhilarating—light, effortless, and fun. He loved the excitement of new connections, the thrill of shared adventures, and the joy of discovering someone new. But inevitably, his partners would want more. More time. More closeness. More vulnerability. Anthony would start to feel suffocated, as if the walls of his carefully constructed world were closing in. He told himself he wasn't avoiding love—he just didn't want to lose the freedom he had worked so hard to protect.

So, he did what he always did when things got too intense: he pulled away. Sometimes, it was subtle—canceling plans last minute, burying himself in work, or booking a solo trip to "clear his head." Other times, it was drastic—an abrupt breakup or a slow, steady withdrawal until the relationship unraveled completely.

Anthony's story isn't unique. If you have avoidant attachment, you might see yourself in his struggle. You might crave connection but fear what it demands of you. It's not that you don't care—it's that vulnerability feels foreign, like a language you were never taught to speak. Deep down, you might wonder: Can I have a

112

healthy, loving relationship without sacrificing the freedom I cherish?

This chapter is about navigating relationships as someone with avoidant attachment—not by forcing yourself to change overnight, but by understanding your patterns, recognizing your triggers, and learning how to build connections without feeling trapped. It's about finding the balance between independence and intimacy, and discovering that love doesn't have to mean losing yourself.

AVOIDANT ATTACHMENT STYLE AND RELATIONSHIPS

Avoidant attachment is commonly misunderstood as a lack of interest in relationships, but the reality is far more nuanced. Individuals with this attachment style usually *desire* connection and intimacy but associate closeness with a perceived loss of independence and control. This creates an internal conflict between a longing for connection and constantly battling a fear of vulnerability. This fear isn't a conscious choice; it's a deeply ingrained response developed in childhood as a protective mechanism.

113

This internal conflict manifests in distinct behavior patterns within adult relationships, creating unique challenges. These challenges often stem from the core fear of being "engulfed" or losing one's sense of self within the relationship. Here's how this plays out in specific behaviors:

1. The Push-Pull of Closeness and Inconsistency:

One of the most defining characteristics of avoidant attachment is the push-pull dynamic. The closer a relationship becomes, the stronger the urge to pull away. This creates inconsistency in behavior, alternating between moments of genuine engagement and sudden withdrawal.

- *Examples:*
    - Being enthusiastic about making plans but then canceling them at the last minute or becoming distant in the days leading up to them.
    - Expressing affection one day and then acting cold and distant the next.

- Engaging in intimate moments but then feeling anxious and needing space afterward.
- Becoming distant after a period of closeness or after a partner expresses vulnerability.

2. Emotional Guarding and Difficulty with Intimacy:

Avoidants build emotional walls to maintain a sense of control and protect against being honest and transparent with your emotions. This makes it difficult to express affection or be physically or emotionally vulnerable.

- *Examples:*
  - Difficulty saying "I love you" or expressing other positive emotions.
  - Avoiding eye contact or physical touch.
  - Deflecting compliments or expressions of love.
  - Changing the subject when conversations become too personal or emotional.

- o Keeping conversations superficial and avoiding deeper discussions about feelings or vulnerabilities.

3. Hyper-Independence and Avoidance of Dependence:

Avoidants highly value self-sufficiency, often equating reliance on others with loss of control or weakness. This mindset can lead them to reject help or support, even in situations where it would genuinely benefit them. The idea of depending on someone—even a trusted partner—can feel unsettling, as if accepting help might erode their independence or create obligations they're not ready for.

- *Examples:*
  - o Turning down financial help, even when struggling - For instance, your significant other offers to cover a bill while you're falling behind on payments, but you refuse—because accepting feels too vulnerable or dependent.

- o Downplaying the need for support or reassurance - You're overwhelmed, but brush it off with, "I'll figure it out," rather than sharing your stress with your partner.
- o Feeling uncomfortable when a partner offers assistance - They offer to pick up groceries, handle a task, or help with something personal, but you reject it instinctively, even if it would make things easier.
- o Prioritizing work, hobbies, or other solo activities over quality time - You choose to stay late at work or dive into a personal project rather than engage in an emotional connection.
- o Resisting financial merging or joint decision-making - Even in a long-term relationship, you hesitate to combine finances or make shared financial commitments, fearing a loss of autonomy.

4. Avoidance of Conflict and Minimizing

Others' Feelings:

Conflict and emotionally charged discussions can trigger feelings of being overwhelmed and a desire to withdraw. Avoidants may also minimize or dismiss their partner's feelings as a way to avoid dealing with the emotional intensity.

- *Examples:*
    - o Withdrawing or becoming silent during arguments.
    - o Changing the subject or deflecting when conflict arises.
    - o Minimizing their partner's concerns or telling them they are overreacting.
    - o Avoiding discussing problems directly or refusing to compromise.
    - o Shutting down emotionally or becoming distant during disagreements.

5. Preference for Casual or Limited Relationships and Prematurely Ending Relationships:

To minimize the risk of emotional engulfment, avoidants may gravitate toward casual relationships or create boundaries in their relationships. When closeness becomes too heavy, they may abruptly end things to regain a sense of freedom.

- *Examples:*
    - Dating long-distance or only seeing someone sporadically.
    - Avoiding labels or commitments.
    - Choosing partners who are emotionally unavailable or already in relationships.
    - Abruptly ending relationships without clear explanation or communication.
    - Creating "tests" for their partner to justify ending the relationship if they "fail."

6. The Cycle of Reinforcement and Emotional Loneliness:

While these avoidant behaviors are intended to protect, they ultimately reinforce the avoidance cycle. The less an avoidant individual experiences the rewards of vulnerability and connection, the stronger

119

their fear of intimacy becomes. This can lead to a deep sense of emotional loneliness and a self-fulfilling prophecy. Additionally, this pattern can hinder emotional growth, making it difficult to progress beyond surface-level interactions and create fulfilling, balanced relationships.

Strategies for Navigating Relationships as an Avoidant

If you recognize these patterns in yourself, remember that change is possible. You can alter your behaviors and create more secure connections with awareness, effort, and the right tools.

Practical Steps:

1. **Develop Self-Awareness:** Understanding your attachment style is the crucial first step. Reflect on how your behaviors affect your relationships and identify areas for improvement.
2. **Challenge Discomfort:** When you feel the urge to withdraw, pause and sit with the discomfort instead of reacting immediately.

Use this time to identify what's triggering your response and consider a small act of connection, like acknowledging your partner's feelings or expressing your need for space in a reassuring way. Over time, this practice helps you build emotional resilience and navigate intimacy without feeling overwhelmed.

3. **Practice Emotional Expression:** Start small by sharing a thought or feeling with someone you trust, gradually increasing your vulnerability.

4. **Cultivate a "We" Mindset:** Shift your focus from individual needs to the needs of the relationship, thinking in terms of "us" and "we."

5. **Seek Professional Support:** Therapy can provide invaluable support in identifying triggers, exploring emotions in a safe space, and developing healthier relational patterns.

6. **Allow Yourself to Feel:** Practice sitting with your emotions without numbing or suppressing them. Acknowledge your desire for connection and allow yourself to explore it.

7. **Engage Your Partner (Appropriately):** Share your journey with your partner in a comfortable way. Involve them in activities that build connection, while also respecting your need for space.

CASE STUDY: MAYA AND CHRIS

Maya had always been fiercely independent, prioritizing her freedom and autonomy above all else. In relationships, she kept things light and casual, avoiding deep emotional conversations at all costs. When she started dating Chris, she was initially drawn to his laid-back personality. However, as their connection deepened and Chris began to express his feelings more openly, Maya felt a growing sense of unease.

For example, when Chris told Maya how much he enjoyed spending time with her and expressed his hopes for a long-term future, Maya's immediate reaction was to pull away. She started canceling plans, citing work commitments and conjuring up excuses, and even contemplated ending the relationship altogether. Internally, she felt a sense of panic, as if she was being cornered or suffocated by his expressions of affection.

Chris, confused and hurt by Maya's sudden distance, eventually confronted her. "I feel like you're pulling away," he said. "Is everything okay?"

Maya's first instinct was to minimize his concerns, saying, "I'm just busy with work," but she remembered her promise to make a change. Instead of deflecting, she took a deep breath and admitted, "It's not you, it's me. I get scared when things get too close."

This small act of vulnerability was a turning point. Maya began seeing a therapist to examine her avoidant tendencies, learning to identify her triggers and develop healthier coping mechanisms. She made a conscious effort to practice sharing small pieces of her emotional world with Chris, expressing her appreciation for his support or acknowledging her own fears.

Over time, Maya learned that vulnerability wasn't about losing control but about gaining a deeper connection. Her relationship with Chris became stronger, grounded on mutual understanding and intentional effort. While she still valued her independence, she also learned to embrace the intimacy and support that a healthy relationship could provide.

Recap: This chapter discussed how avoidant attachment manifests in relationships and provided practical strategies for navigating these challenges. You've learned about common avoidant behaviors, the push-pull dynamic, and actionable steps to build healthier connections. In the next chapter, we'll focus on understanding and supporting a partner with avoidant attachment, offering practical tools for building empathy and fostering deeper connections from your partner's perspective.

Key Points to Remember:

- Avoidant behaviors like distancing, avoiding conflict, and prioritizing independence can create barriers in relationships.
- Emotional closeness feels risky but is essential for building trust and intimacy.

- Progress happens gradually—small, intentional steps lead to meaningful connections.

Reflect on how avoidant tendencies may have impacted your relationships. What steps can you take to stay engaged and build trust with those you care about?

CHAPTER 5: LOVING AND SUPPORTING AN AVOIDANT PARTNER

"A relationship is about two people holding space for one another's humanity, fears, and flaws while building something stronger together." – Unknown

Imagine this: You're standing on the shore of a lake, calling out to someone in a boat just a few feet away. They're close enough to hear you, but no matter how much you reach out, they keep rowing backward, maintaining the same distance. You're not asking for much—just a little closeness, a little connection. But every time you step forward, they drift further away.

This might feel all too familiar if you're in a relationship with someone with avoidant attachment. You're not alone in this struggle. I remember working with a couple—let's call them Mia and Jake. Mia was warm, expressive, and eager to connect, while Jake was thoughtful, independent, and fiercely protective of his space. At first, their differences seemed complementary. But over time, Mia began to feel like she was chasing someone who didn't want to be caught. On the other hand, Jake felt like no matter how much he cared, he was constantly being asked to give more than he could.

The truth is, loving someone with avoidant attachment can feel like a paradox. They may deeply value the relationship, yet their actions can leave you feeling unseen, unheard, or even unwanted. It's not that they don't care; vulnerability feels like stepping into uncharted territory, and self-protection becomes their default setting.

This chapter isn't about fixing your partner or changing who they are. It's about understanding their world, learning how to navigate their unique needs, and creating a relationship where both of you feel safe,

128

seen, and valued. Together, we'll explore how to bridge the gap between closeness and independence, and how to support your partner's growth without losing yourself in the process.

WHAT AVOIDANT ATTACHMENT LOOKS LIKE IN A PARTNER

Partners with avoidant attachment often exhibit behaviors that may feel confusing, frustrating, or even hurtful. However, these behaviors are rarely about a lack of love or commitment—they're self-protective mechanisms developed over time to avoid vulnerability.

Common Behaviors of an Avoidant Partner

- Discomfort with Closeness: They may seem uneasy with emotional intimacy, often deflecting or avoiding vulnerable conversations.
- Inconsistent Engagement: Your partner might alternate between moments of affection and withdrawal, leaving you unsure of where you stand.

- Prioritization of Independence: They highly value their autonomy and may resist reliance on others or being relied upon.
- Difficulty Expressing Emotions: Avoidants often struggle to articulate their feelings, leading to misunderstandings.
- Avoidance of Conflict: They may sidestep difficult conversations, choosing to shut down rather than address issues head-on.

WHY AVOIDANTS BEHAVE THIS WAY

Understanding the root of avoidant behaviors is essential for building empathy and fostering a healthier relationship. Here's what might be happening beneath the surface:

The Longing for Connection and the Fear of It

Avoidants have feelings and desire meaningful connections, but their fear of vulnerability is equally strong. Past experiences of emotional shut-down or dismissal can reinforce the belief that vulnerability leads to rejection.

The Normalization of Independence

Independence, solitude, and isolation are often normalized for avoidants, becoming survival strategies. Over time, they may even take pride in their self-reliance, seeing it as a strength. This perspective allows them to feel empowered within their reality, even if it means sacrificing emotional closeness.

Connection Triggers Their Nervous System

Emotional closeness and intensity can trigger the fight/flight/freeze response in avoidants. They may have learned in childhood that strong emotions were "dangerous" or unacceptable. They learned that when emotions ran high, something was "wrong," so they shut down or withdrew as a protective mechanism.

For example, when an avoidant partner witnesses their partner expressing strong emotions, they might say things like:

- "Calm down; this isn't that big of a deal."
- "Why are you yelling right now?"

131

- "I can't talk to you when you're upset like this—
  go calm down, and then we can talk."

These responses might seem dismissive in the heat of emotional exchanges, but they actually reveal the avoidant partner's inner turmoil and panic. This sets off the anxious-avoidant cycle: the avoidant pulls away, the anxious partner chases them, and both parties end up feeling more disconnected and upset.

Shutting Down is Internal Panic

When your avoidant partner shuts down, they are not emotionally unaffected. On the outside, they may appear indifferent or dismissive, but internally, they are struggling with fear and feeling overwhelmed. Their outward calmness is a defense mechanism to manage the emotional chaos they feel inside.

Difficulty Naming and Recognizing Emotions

Avoidants often struggle to identify or even recognize their feelings. In their upbringing, emotions may have been dismissed or invalidated, leading them to internalize the belief that their feelings were unwelcome. Over time, they learned to compartmentalize their emotions and operate primarily from a place of logic and reason, spending more time in their minds than their hearts.

Superficial Interactions as Self-Protection

Avoidants often engage in self-protective behaviors that keep relationships at a superficial level to avoid potential pain. Their past experiences with closeness may have been agonizing, and enduring that suffering once more doesn't feel like an option. As a result, they keep conversations light, avoid emotional depth, and shy away from situations that expose their true feelings.

Commitment and the Fear of Being Trapped

Commitment is particularly challenging for avoidants because it removes their perceived "exit plan." To them, commitment is associated with vulnerability, intimacy, and the messiness of human relationships— all of which can feel daunting. The idea of being tied to a situation without a way out can lead to hesitation or resistance to long-term commitments like marriage or moving in together.

Understanding these underlying dynamics allows you to view your partner's behaviors with empathy rather than frustration. Their actions are about self-protection, not a rejection of you.

ARE WE DOOMED?

Relationships with avoidants can be challenging, but they are not doomed. You may sometimes feel like the odds are stacked against you. Their tendency to withdraw or put up emotional walls can leave you feeling isolated, frustrated, and even doubt your worth in the relationship. But here's the encouraging part— individuals with *avoidant attachment can change.*

Avoidant partners are capable of love and connection—they're often deeply yearning for it, but their fear of vulnerability creates insurmountable barriers. That wall you feel? It's not just blocking you; it's holding them captive too. They may want to step out of the fortress they've built, but they need safety and patience to do so.

134

Threatening, badgering, or making demands of an avoidant partner will likely backfire. These individuals may appear tough and self-sufficient but can feel threatened easily. If you consistently offer safety and understanding, your partner will slowly start to step out of their shell and open up. This won't happen overnight—it's a long game requiring patience, empathy, and mutual effort.

How to Tell If an Avoidant Loves You

People often wonder, "Do avoidants even feel love?" or think, "What's the point in expressing my affection if they don't reciprocate it in the same way?"

The truth is, avoidants express love differently. Their affection might not show up in traditional ways, like frequent declarations of love or grand romantic gestures. Instead, avoidants typically express their love through subtle and indirect actions. If you're wondering whether your avoidant partner loves you, look for these signs:

SIX SIGNS AN AVOIDANT PARTNER LOVES YOU

1. Indirect Signs of Affection

Avoidants may struggle to express emotions verbally, but their love often comes through in nonverbal ways. They might show affection with warm smiles, a lingering touch, or extended eye contact during special moments.

2. Looser Boundaries

Avoidants are known for maintaining strict personal boundaries, but as they feel more secure in the relationship, they may lower these walls little by little. This could mean inviting you into aspects of their life they usually keep private or becoming more receptive to your involvement in their routines.

- Tip: Be patient. This process may take time, and it's not uncommon for avoidants to temporarily regress by reestablishing some boundaries.

3. Displays of Vulnerability

Exposing their inner world can be deeply uncomfortable. If your partner begins to share their thoughts, emotions, or fears with you, even in small doses, it's a significant sign of trust and love. These moments of vulnerability are their way of saying they feel safe with you.

4. Attention to Your Needs

Avoidants might not always respond promptly to your wants and needs, but if they listen carefully and consider your preferences, it shows they care. For example, they may surprise you with something they know you like or adjust their behavior to accommodate your feelings.

- Tip: When they do something thoughtful, acknowledge it with praise or gratitude. Positive reinforcement encourages them to continue these loving actions.

5. Sharing Activities

Avoidants are fiercely independent and prefer to engage in hobbies and activities independently. If they invite you to join them in something they usually enjoy solo—like a favorite sport, creative project, or a fun outing—it's a strong indicator that they're forging a deeper connection with you. Including you in their interests is their way of drawing you closer.

6. Considering Psychological Guidance

One of the most evident signs an avoidant partner loves you is their willingness to work on the relationship through therapy. Since avoidants dislike discussing emotions, agreeing to pursue individual or couples counseling is a major step for them. It demonstrates their commitment to processing their feelings and addressing challenges for the sake of your connection.

Loving an avoidant partner requires attentiveness, patience, and an appreciation for subtle expressions of affection. While they may not wear their heart on their sleeve, their love is evident in the ways they lower their guard, involve you in their world, and work toward building trust. By understanding how avoidants express their feelings, you can appreciate the depth of their emotions and strengthen your bond with them.

10 GUIDING PRINCIPLES FOR SUPPORTING AN AVOIDANT PARTNER

Supporting a partner with avoidant attachment doesn't mean trying to fix them or fundamentally change who they are. Supporting an avoidant partner means creating an empathetic space where they can process their emotions without fear. Here's how:

1. Understand Their Attachment Style

The first step is to understand your partner's avoidant tendencies. Recognize that their behaviors are rooted in fear of vulnerability, not a lack of love.

By learning how their childhood experiences shaped their attachment style, you can reframe their actions in a more empathetic light. Instead of feeling hurt or frustrated, you'll see their behavior as a reflection of their internal struggles, not a rejection of your relationship.

2. Understand your own attachment style

Recognizing your own attachment style helps you understand your reactions to your partner's behavior. Each attachment style is associated with unique traits, which can affect the compatibility between partners in a relationship.

For example, two avoidants in a relationship may get along well since they both respect each other's need for space and discomfort with expressing emotions. However, someone with an anxious attachment style in relationships may struggle to understand an avoidant partner's actions and push for closeness.

3. Don't Chase Them

When they shut down or pull away, your instinct might be to press harder, hoping they'll open up. However, chasing them will likely cause them to retreat even further. Avoidants are experts at self-reliance and tend to value their independence highly. They often need to feel in control of their engagement in a relationship.

Instead of chasing, let your partner know you're available when they're ready to talk. This approach allows them to feel safe and respected, reducing their anxiety about losing autonomy. For example, you might say:

- "I can tell you're feeling overwhelmed, and I'm here whenever you're ready to talk."

This reassurance signals that you're a trustworthy and dependable presence in their life without imposing your timeline.

4. Be Steady and Reliable

Trust is one of the biggest hurdles for avoidants. Their tendency to rely on themselves means they find it hard to depend on others. Building trust requires consistency in both your words and actions.

Here's how you can create a sense of reliability:

- Follow through on promises, no matter how small.
- Show up consistently, even during times when your partner pulls away.

- Remind your partner—both verbally and through actions—that their needs matter to you.

5. Respond Without Judgment

When your partner begins to open up, how you respond is critical. Avoidants are cautious about vulnerability because they fear judgment, criticism, or rejection. If they share something personal, resist the urge to fix, criticize, or minimize their feelings.

Avoid phrases like:

- "Why can't you just open up like other people?"
- "I don't understand why you're like this."

Instead, validate their efforts and feelings. For example:

- "Thank you for sharing that with me. I know it's not easy, and I really appreciate your openness."
- "I can see that this is hard for you to talk about, and I really respect that you're sharing this with me."

Validation reinforces their willingness to engage emotionally and builds trust over time.

6. Give Them Time and Space

Avoidants process emotions differently than others. After opening up, they may feel a momentary sense of relief, but that relief can quickly be followed by a need to withdraw.

For avoidants, vulnerability can feel overwhelming, exposing, or even destabilizing. Their instinctive response is to retreat to regain a sense of stability.

Instead of taking this withdrawal personally or pressuring them to stay emotionally engaged, allow them the space they need while reassuring them that connection is still available.

For example, you might say:

- "I know this is a lot for you to process, and I'm here whenever you want to talk more."
- "Take whatever time you need—I just want you to know I'm not going anywhere."

143

This balance of patience and presence creates a secure base for your partner, making it easier for them to return to connection on their terms—without fear of being judged or suffocated. Over time, this consistent reassurance helps them feel safe enough to remain engaged for longer periods without retreating.

7. Frame Vulnerability as a Shared Journey

Avoidants often view vulnerability as something that makes them weak or exposes them to risk. To help your partner see vulnerability differently, frame it as a shared journey rather than an individual task.

This collaborative approach reduces their fear of "attempting it alone" and helps them feel supported in building a deeper connection.

8. Recognize That It's Not About You

One of the hardest lessons when loving an avoidant partner is recognizing their behavior is not about you. Their silence, withdrawal, or hesitation to engage doesn't reflect your worth or the value of your relationship. It's about their internal struggles.

144

When you stop taking their actions personally, you free yourself from disappointment and insecurity. This perspective allows you to respond with compassion and patience rather than defensiveness or blame.

9. Encourage Communication Gently

Encourage your partner to share their thoughts and feelings, but do so gently. Avoidants often struggle to articulate their emotions, fearing being misunderstood or judged. When they do open up, acknowledge their courage and validate their experience.

For example:

- "I know it's hard for you to share how you feel, and I really appreciate you trusting me with this."

Acknowledging their effort helps build confidence and reinforces the safety of your relationship as a space for emotional connection.

10. Seek Professional Support Together

Working with a therapist can be a transformative experience if both partners are willing. A skilled therapist can provide a neutral space for exploring attachment challenges and help you develop strategies to support each other more effectively. Therapy also allows your avoidant partner to unpack their attachment triggers and build healthier ways of connecting.

STRATEGIES FOR BUILDING A STRONGER RELATIONSHIP

Building a fulfilling relationship with an avoidantly attached partner presents unique challenges, but it's absolutely achievable. The key lies in understanding their underlying fears and adapting your approach to create a safe and supportive environment. This involves effective communication, building trust and security, respecting their need for space, and encouraging gradual vulnerability.

CULTIVATING EFFECTIVE COMMUNICATION

Communication is the cornerstone of any healthy relationship, but with an avoidant partner, it requires extra care and effort. The way you communicate can either invite connection or provoke their defenses.

- **Prioritize Calm and Composed Communication:** Avoid emotional intensity, especially during sensitive conversations. Maintaining a calm and soothing tone creates a sense of safety and reduces the likelihood of triggering their withdrawal response. If you find yourself becoming emotionally charged, take a break to regulate your emotions before continuing the conversation.

- **Focus on "I" Statements and Shared Experiences:** Frame your communication around your feelings and experiences rather than placing blame or making accusations. Instead of saying, "You never talk about your feelings," try, "I sometimes feel disconnected when we don't share our thoughts and feelings, and I'd love to find ways to connect more deeply." This approach encourages dialogue without making your partner feel cornered or criticized.

- **Employ Open-Ended Questions and Active Listening:** Avoid questions that feel like interrogations or demands. Instead, use open-ended questions that invite your partner to share their thoughts and feelings at their own pace. For example, rather than asking, "Why are you so distant?" try, "I've noticed you seem a bit quieter lately. Is there anything you'd like to talk about?" When your partner does share, practice active listening by truly hearing what they are saying, reflecting on their words, and validating their perspective, even if you don't entirely agree.

- **Validate Their Feelings and Experiences:** Validation is crucial for building trust with an avoidant partner. Even if you don't understand or agree with their perspective, acknowledge their feelings and show that you respect their experience. For example, if your partner feels overwhelmed by a social event, you could say, "I understand that large gatherings can be draining. It makes sense that you'd need some time to recharge afterward." This reassures them that their feelings are valid and that you're not trying to dismiss or change their perspective.

BUILDING TRUST AND FOSTERING SECURITY

Trust is essential for any relationship, but it's particularly crucial for avoidant partners, who often struggle with trusting others due to past experiences. Building trust requires patience and consistency while creating a safe environment.

- **Demonstrate Consistent Reliability and Follow-Through:** Consistency in your actions and words is paramount. Follow through on promises, even small ones, and show up consistently, even when your partner pulls away. This demonstrates that you are a dependable and trustworthy presence in their life. For example, if you say you'll call at a certain time, make sure you do. If you make plans, honor them. These small acts of consistency build trust over time.

- **Create a Safe and Non-Judgmental Space:** Approach conversations with curiosity and empathy, not confrontation or criticism. Avoid making judgments about their feelings or behaviors. Instead, create a space where they feel safe to express themselves without fear of being criticized or dismissed. If they do open up, even in small ways, acknowledge their courage and express your appreciation.

- **Celebrate Small Steps and Progress:** Building trust and intimacy with an avoidant partner is a gradual process. Celebrate small victories, such as moments of vulnerability or increased engagement. Acknowledge their efforts and express your appreciation for their willingness to connect. This positive reinforcement encourages them to continue taking steps toward greater intimacy.

RESPECTING THEIR NEED FOR SPACE AND AUTONOMY:

One of the most important aspects of supporting an avoidant partner is respecting their need for space and autonomy. Avoidants often feel overwhelmed by too much closeness, so giving them the necessary breathing room is crucial.

- **Balance Space with Connection:** While respecting their need for space, maintaining connection is also essential. Find a balance between giving them space to recharge and creating opportunities for meaningful interaction. This might involve scheduling regular date nights or simply checking in with a thoughtful text message.

- **Reassure Them of Their Independence:** Make sure to reassure your partner that your love and desire for connection doesn't mean you want to control them or take away their independence. Emphasize that you value their autonomy and respect their need for personal space.

- **Encourage but Don't Force Vulnerability:** Encourage your partner to share their feelings, but avoid pressuring them to open up before they are ready. Let them take the lead in deciding when and how to express their emotions. Pushing them will likely backfire and cause them to withdraw further.

NORMALIZING VULNERABILITY AND LEADING BY EXAMPLE:

One of the most powerful ways to encourage vulnerability in an avoidant partner is to normalize it through your own actions.

- **Share Your Own Vulnerabilities (Appropriately):** By sharing your feelings, fears, and struggles in a healthy and appropriate way, you demonstrate that vulnerability is safe and can lead to deeper connection. This encourages your partner to take small steps toward openness, but be mindful not to inundate them with your emotions or expect them to provide all the emotional support.

- **Reframe Emotional Expression as a Shared Journey:** Frame emotional discussions and vulnerability as a collaborative effort rather than a weakness. Emphasize that you're in this together and willing to support one another. This helps reduce their fear of "going it alone" and encourages them to view openness as a shared opportunity for growth.

Integrating these strategies into your relationship can create a more supportive and understanding dynamic that honors both partners' needs. Remember that progress takes time and patience, but you can build a stronger and more fulfilling connection with consistent effort and empathy.

CASE STUDY: MARK AND RACHEL

Mark and Rachel had been together for three years when Rachel noticed a pattern: during deep conversations or arguments, Mark would shut down and withdraw, leaving Rachel feeling unheard. Rachel learned about avoidant attachment and realized Mark's distancing wasn't personal. She began creating small opportunities for connection, respecting his need for space while sharing her own feelings calmly. Over time, Mark felt more comfortable expressing himself, strengthening their bond. Mark now admits, "I still struggle with opening up, but Rachel's patience has shown me I can trust her. It's a work in progress, but we're building something solid."

REFLECTION EXERCISE

Take a moment to reflect on your relationship:

- What behaviors or patterns do you recognize in your avoidant partner?
- How have those behaviors impacted your relationship?
- What small steps could you take to create a more supportive and empathetic dynamic?

Recap: This chapter provided insights into understanding and supporting an avoidant partner. You learned about common avoidant behaviors, their underlying causes, and practical strategies for a healthier dynamic. In the next chapter, we'll shift the focus to actionable strategies for avoidants to move toward secure attachment, enabling them to embrace vulnerability and build deeper connections.

Key Points to Remember:

- Avoidant partners often equate vulnerability with loss of control—patience and empathy are key.

- Pushing or chasing can backfire; instead, offer support and create a sense of safety.
- Open communication and consistent actions help build trust and foster deeper connection.

CHAPTER 6: MOVING TOWARD SECURE ATTACHMENT

"Healing doesn't mean the damage never existed. It means the damage no longer controls our lives." –
Unknown

Imagine a relationship where you feel deeply connected, confident, and unconditionally loved. A space where you can be yourself, trust comes naturally, and communication flows effortlessly. This vision of secure attachment might seem like a distant dream, especially if your childhood experiences haven't provided a solid foundation.

However, moving toward secure attachment is a transformative journey. It requires unlearning deeply ingrained habits of fear and avoidance, embracing vulnerability, and building trust in yourself and others. This chapter explores the key elements of secure attachment, how it develops, and how you can cultivate it in your own life, even if your past experiences haven't always been ideal.

THE FOUNDATION OF SECURE ATTACHMENT

Secure attachment begins in childhood, nurtured by a consistent and responsive caregiving environment. When a child's emotional, physical, and mental needs are consistently met, they learn to trust that their needs are important and will be addressed.

Key elements of this secure foundation include:

- **Attuned Caregivers:** When a child experiences distress, a responsive caregiver acknowledges their emotions, provides comfort, and offers reassurance. This teaches the child that their feelings are valid and that they can rely on others for support.

- **Emotional Validation:** Caregivers who validate a child's emotions – even anger, sadness, or fear – build a foundation of trust and security. The child learns that their feelings are important and that they can express themselves freely without fear of judgment or rejection.

While a nurturing childhood provides an ideal foundation, secure attachment isn't solely determined by early experiences. With self-awareness, intentional effort, and supportive relationships, anyone can cultivate secure attachment patterns, regardless of their past.

CHARACTERISTICS OF SECURE ATTACHMENT

Secure attachment lays the groundwork for a relationship where both partners feel valued, understood, and empowered to thrive individually and as a team. People with this style exhibit several key traits:

- Emotional Intelligence and Responsiveness: They recognize and regulate their emotions while empathizing with others.
- Effective Conflict Management: They address disagreements constructively without fear that conflict will threaten the relationship.
- Comfort with Intimacy: They embrace emotional closeness and vulnerability.
- Trusting and Reliable: They trust others and are dependable in their actions.
- Open Communication: They clearly express their emotions and needs while being considerate of their partner's feelings.
- Balanced Self-View: They hold a positive self-image and accept that they are worthy of love.
- Supportive and Generous: They offer support and care without becoming overly self-sacrificing or codependent.

DISTINGUISHING SECURE ATTACHMENT FROM INSECURE STYLES

The core difference between securely attached individuals and those with insecure attachment styles lies in their ability to navigate emotions and relationships without getting stuck in harmful cycles. While everyone experiences a full spectrum of emotions—joy, sadness, anger, fear—securely attached individuals have a fundamentally different relationship with these feelings. They don't perceive emotions, especially negative ones, as threats to the relationship or sense of identity. Instead, they view them as valuable insights, opportunities for connection, and catalysts for personal growth.

Here's a deeper look at how this difference manifests:

- **Emotional Regulation and Perspective:** Securely attached individuals possess a strong capacity for emotional regulation. They understand that emotions are temporary states, not permanent reflections of their worth or the state of their relationship. This allows them to maintain perspective during emotionally charged moments and avoid overreacting or becoming overwhelmed. In contrast, insecurely attached individuals may struggle with emotional regulation, leading to reactive behaviors such as:

- o **Anxious Attachment:** Heightened emotional reactivity, seeking constant reassurance, and fearing abandonment.
- o **Avoidant Attachment:** Suppressing or minimizing emotions, withdrawing from intimacy, and dreading engulfment.
- **Open Communication and Vulnerability:** Securely attached individuals are comfortable expressing their emotions and needs openly and honestly. They trust that their partner will respond with empathy and care, even when discussing difficult or vulnerable topics. This fosters a sense of safety and intimacy within the relationship. Insecurely attached individuals, on the other hand, often struggle with open communication:
  - o **Anxious Attachment:** Communicating their needs in a demanding or anxious way, seeking constant validation and reassurance.
  - o **Avoidant Attachment:** Avoiding expressing their needs altogether, fearing vulnerability and rejection.
- **Conflict Resolution and Repair:** Conflict is inevitable in any relationship. Securely attached

individuals view conflict as an opportunity for growth and connection. They approach disagreements with a desire to understand their partner's perspective, find mutually agreeable solutions, and repair any emotional damage that may have occurred. This process of "rupture and repair" strengthens the bond and deepens trust. Insecurely attached individuals may approach conflict in less constructive ways:

- **Anxious Attachment:** Becoming too emotional, clingy, or accusatory during conflict, fearing that the disagreement will lead to abandonment.

- **Avoidant Attachment:** Withdrawing, shutting down, or becoming defensive during conflict, avoiding emotional involvement.

- **Trust and Reliance:** Securely attached individuals have a basic sense of trust in their partner and the relationship's stability. They are comfortable relying on their partner for support during difficult times and offering support in return. This mutual reliance fosters a sense of interdependence, where both partners feel secure and supported while maintaining their individuality. Insecurely attached individuals may struggle with trust and reliance:

- ○ **Anxious Attachment:** Difficulty trusting their partner's love and commitment, constantly seeking reassurance, and fearing betrayal.

- ○ **Avoidant Attachment:** They may have difficulty relying on others, preferring to handle everything on their own and viewing reliance as a weakness.

In essence, secure attachment allows individuals to experience the full range of human emotions without letting those feelings dictate their behavior or jeopardize the stability of their relationships. They can navigate the complexities of intimacy, conflict, and interdependence with confidence and resilience, fostering deeper and more fulfilling connections. On the other hand, insecure attachment leads to emotional dysregulation and maladaptive relationship patterns that hinder the ability to form true intimacy and connection.

THE JOURNEY TOWARD SECURE ATTACHMENT

Developing a secure attachment isn't about erasing past experiences or striving for perfection. Instead, it involves cultivating the tools, habits, and mindset that empower you to navigate relationships with confidence, emotional stability, and genuine connection. Secure attachment is a process of growth and transformation, and it begins with intentional steps toward self-awareness, emotional regulation, and trust-building.

STEP 1: UNDERSTANDING YOUR ATTACHMENT STYLE

Understanding your current attachment style is the foundation of moving toward secure attachment. This self-exploration provides clarity on how your past has influenced your present and helps you identify areas for growth.

Reflect on Your Childhood Experiences

Our attachment styles often originate from childhood interactions with caregivers. Reflect on:

- Were your emotional needs met consistently?

165

- Did you feel safe expressing vulnerability?
- How did your caregivers respond to your distress?

For example, if you grew up in an environment where your emotions were dismissed, you may have developed avoidant tendencies to protect yourself from rejection. Alternatively, if your caregivers were inconsistent, you might lean toward anxious attachment, always seeking reassurance.

Examine Patterns in Past Relationships

Are there recurring themes in your relationships, such as fear of abandonment, difficulty with trust, or emotional withdrawal? These patterns can provide valuable insights into your attachment tendencies.

Identify Emotional Triggers

Pay attention to the situations that evoke strong emotional reactions, such as jealousy, rejection, or criticism. Understanding what triggers these feelings helps you recognize when your attachment style is influencing your behavior.

STEP 2: CULTIVATING SELF-AWARENESS AND EMOTIONAL REGULATION

Self-awareness and emotional regulation are critical skills for developing secure attachment. These tools enable you to understand and manage your emotions, minimizing reactive behaviors that can put a strain on relationships.

Developing Self-Awareness

Self-awareness involves tuning into your thoughts, emotions, and reactions. Mindfulness practices can help:

- Journaling: Write about your daily experiences and emotional responses. Over time, this can reveal patterns in your thoughts and behaviors.
- Meditation: Focus on the present moment without judgment. This practice helps you observe your emotions as they arise, creating space for intentional responses.

Practicing Emotional Regulation

Emotional regulation allows you to manage intense feelings without becoming overwhelmed or reactive. Try these strategies:

- Deep Breathing: Slow, intentional breathing calms your nervous system. Inhale for four counts, hold for four, and exhale for four.
- Pause and Reflect: When emotions run high, pause before responding. Ask yourself: What am I feeling? Why am I feeling this way? How can I respond constructively?

STEP 3: CHALLENGING NEGATIVE BELIEFS

Negative beliefs about yourself or relationships often underlie insecure attachment. These beliefs may stem from past experiences and perpetuate feelings of unworthiness or mistrust. It's essential to identify and challenge these thoughts to move toward secure attachment.

Identify Your Negative Beliefs

Pay attention to recurring self-critical or limiting thoughts, such as:

- "I'm not lovable."
- "People always let me down."

Reframe and Replace

Examine the origins of these beliefs—did they come from childhood experiences, past relationships, or societal messages? Once you've identified their source, work to reframe them. For example:

- Replace "I'm not lovable" with "I am worthy of love and connection."
- Replace "People always let me down" with "I can set boundaries and choose relationships that support me."

Over time, these positive affirmations reshape your perception of yourself and others, paving the way for healthier interactions.

STEP 4: PRACTICING EFFECTIVE COMMUNICATION AND SETTING HEALTHY BOUNDARIES

Secure attachment thrives on clear communication and well-defined boundaries. These skills foster trust, respect, and emotional intimacy in relationships.

Communicate Openly and Respectfully

Express your needs and feelings without fear of judgment or rejection. Use "I" statements to take ownership of your emotions and avoid placing blame. For example:

- Instead of saying, "You never listen to me," try: "I feel unheard when I share my thoughts, and I'd appreciate it if we could focus on listening to each other more."

Set and Maintain Healthy Boundaries

Boundaries protect your emotional well-being while fostering respect in relationships. Clearly communicate your limits and enforce them with consistency. For example:

- If you need alone time to recharge, let your partner know: "I need some time to myself after work to relax. Let's connect later this evening."

STEP 5: BUILDING TRUST AND SECURITY

Surround yourself with individuals who demonstrate secure attachment traits, and work to embody those traits yourself.

Cultivate Reliability

Show up for your loved ones in meaningful ways, such as keeping promises, offering support, and being present during difficult times.

Engage in Shared Activities

Strengthen your bonds by engaging in activities that foster connection and collaboration. For example:

- Plan a trip together.
- Take a class to learn something new as a team.
- Establish regular rituals, like weekly date nights or shared meals.

Offer Reassurance

Regularly remind your loved ones that their emotions and needs matter to you. For example:

- "I see that you're upset, and I want you to know I'm here to support you."

Secure attachment focuses on resilience, adaptability, and navigating relationships authentically and confidently. Each step brings you closer to the emotional freedom and connection you deserve.

WHAT SECURE ATTACHMENT LOOKS LIKE IN RELATIONSHIPS

Let's analyze the key characteristics of secure attachment in relationships and how they contribute to a thriving partnership.

Rupture and Repair: Turning Conflict into Connection

Conflict is inevitable in any relationship, but securely attached couples handle disagreements differently. Instead of avoiding, escalating, or becoming stuck in a cycle of blame, they see conflict as an opportunity to strengthen their bond.

- The Concept of Rupture: A "rupture" occurs when a misunderstanding, disagreement, or hurt feeling disrupts the flow of connection between partners. This is normal and happens in even the healthiest relationships.
- The Importance of Repair: What sets securely attached couples apart is their ability to repair after a rupture. They approach the conflict with a willingness to listen, empathize, and find common ground.

Example: After an argument, one partner might say, "I'm sorry for snapping at you earlier. I was feeling stressed, but that doesn't excuse my behavior. Can we talk about what happened?" This effort to acknowledge hurt and take responsibility creates an environment where both partners feel respected and understood.

Repairing a rift requires humility, patience, and mutual effort. By addressing issues directly and with empathy, securely attached partners strengthen their connection and build trust.

Mutual Growth: Evolving Together

In secure relationships, partners can grow, evolve, and support each other. This growth isn't one-sided; it's a dynamic process where both people contribute to and benefit from the relationship.

- Encouraging Each Other's Goals: In secure relationships, partners celebrate each other's ambitions and provide support without jealousy or fear of being left behind.
- Learning Through Differences: Differences in perspective or personality are seen as opportunities to expand understanding rather than sources of conflict.

Example: If one partner decides to pursue a new career path, the other might offer encouragement, discuss potential challenges, and brainstorm ways to make the transition smoother. This collaborative approach fosters a sense of partnership and shared success.

Mutual growth also involves recognizing that both partners will change over time. Securely attached individuals view these changes not as threats but as

174

natural parts of life, allowing them to adapt and deepen their connection as they evolve together.

Balanced Independence: Connection Without Losing Yourself

One of the hallmarks of secure attachment is the ability to maintain a balance between connection and independence. Securely attached partners can rely on each other for support while still preserving their individuality.

- Healthy Interdependence: In a secure relationship, partners are comfortable leaning on each other during difficult times without becoming overly dependent. They know they can trust their partner to be there when needed but also feel confident in their own ability to handle challenges.
- Maintaining Individuality: Secure attachment allows both partners to pursue their own interests, friendships, and hobbies without worrying about drifting apart.

Example: A securely attached couple might spend a weekend pursuing separate activities—one attending a yoga retreat and the other catching up with friends— then spend time together afterward.

Emotional Safety

Both partners feel comfortable expressing their thoughts, needs, and vulnerabilities without fear of judgment or rejection.

Effective Communication

Secure partners communicate openly, actively listen, and validate each other's feelings, even when they don't fully agree.

Shared Responsibility

Tasks, decisions, and emotional labor are shared fairly, creating a sense of partnership and equity.

Resilience in Adversity

Secure relationships can weather life's challenges, from job losses to health issues, by leaning on each other for support.

MINDSET SHIFTS FOR SECURE ATTACHMENT

Cultivating secure attachment also requires transforming your perspective on relationships. The beliefs and assumptions you hold about yourself, your partner, and the nature of relationships profoundly shape how you engage with others. By adjusting your mindset, you create a foundation for healthier, more fulfilling connections.

1. Embrace Growth

Secure relationships thrive on growth—not just as individuals but as partners navigating life together. Viewing your relationship as a dynamic, evolving entity allows you to see challenges not as setbacks but as opportunities for learning and development.

- Shift Your Perspective: Instead of fearing change, embrace it as a natural part of any relationship. Recognize that both you and your partner will grow and adapt over time, and this evolution can deepen your bond if you're willing to navigate it together.

- Example: If your partner expresses a new interest or perspective that feels unfamiliar, instead of resisting it, approach it with curiosity. Ask questions like, "What sparked this interest?" or "How can I support you in exploring this?" This openness fosters mutual growth.

Focusing on growth doesn't mean avoiding challenges—it means leaning into them with the confidence that you and your partner can work through them together. Each resolved conflict, compromise, or shared milestone strengthens the foundation of your relationship.

2. Celebrate Differences

Differences in personality, background, or attachment style can sometimes feel like obstacles. However, these differences are opportunities to learn more about each other and to develop empathy, adaptability, and patience.

- Reframe Differences as Strengths: Recognize that your partner's unique traits bring balance and perspective to the relationship. For example, if you're naturally expressive and your partner is more reserved, their calm demeanor can help ground you during moments of heightened emotion.
- Collaborative Problem-Solving: When differences arise, tackle them as a team. Use language that emphasizes partnership, such as, "How can we navigate this together?" rather than, "Why can't you just understand?"

Celebrating differences can change how you perceive them. Instead of seeing them as causes of conflict, you can start acknowledging them as opportunities for enrichment. Each partner's diverse experiences, thoughts, and feelings can create a vibrant, balanced relationship that celebrates individuality.

3. Release Perfectionism

One of the most liberating shifts in mindset for cultivating secure attachment is letting go of perfectionism. Relationships are not meant to be flawless, and neither you nor your partner need to be perfect to create a fulfilling connection.

- Focus on Resilience: Secure attachment isn't about avoiding conflict or never making mistakes. It's about learning how to repair after disagreements, forgive missteps, and move forward together. Trust and connection grow stronger when both partners are willing to engage in the "rupture and repair" process.
- Accept Imperfections: Both you and your partner will have moments of insecurity, miscommunication, or frustration. Instead of seeing these as failures, view them as part of the normal ebb and flow of a relationship.
- Adopt a Growth Mindset: Shift your focus from "What's wrong?" to "What can we learn from this?" This approach encourages collaboration and reduces the fear of making mistakes.

- Be Kind to Yourself and Your Partner: Practice self-compassion when you fall short of your own expectations. Extend the same grace to your partner. For example, if they forget an important date, instead of lashing out, consider saying, "I know you care about me, even if this slipped your mind."

Letting go of perfectionism allows you to focus on the heart of your relationship—connection, trust, and shared growth—rather than pursuing unrealistic ideals.

SHIFTING YOUR MINDSET IN ACTION

Transforming your mindset requires consistent effort and intentionality. Here's how you can start:

- Practice Reflection: At the end of each day, ask yourself: "How did I approach my relationship today? Did I embrace growth, celebrate differences, or release perfectionism?"
- Model Vulnerability: Share your mindset shifts with your partner. For example, you might say: "I've been working on letting go of

perfectionism, so I want to acknowledge how much I appreciate the effort you put into resolving that disagreement earlier."

- Seek Feedback: Invite your partner to share their thoughts on how they view your efforts. This creates a collaborative environment where both of you can grow together.

Transforming your mindset opens the door to a healthier, more enriching emotional landscape for yourself and your partner. Let these shifts guide you toward deeper trust, empathy, and connection as you continue your journey toward secure attachment.

CASE STUDY: EMILY AND JAKE

Emily and Jake have been together for five years. When Jake unexpectedly loses his job, he initially withdraws, feeling embarrassed and unsure how to express his emotions. Emily notices his change in behavior and gently initiates a conversation. "I've noticed you've seemed distant lately. I want you to know I'm here for you, no matter what happens."

This encourages Jake to open up about his fears of failure and uncertainty about the future. Instead of trying to "fix" the situation, Emily listens, validates his feelings, and asks how she can support him. Together, they brainstorm ways to manage their finances and explore job opportunities.

This interaction demonstrates secure attachment in action: Emily's emotional availability and Jake's willingness to open up create a safe space for connection, even in the face of adversity.

Recap: This chapter explored the journey toward secure attachment, providing practical steps and mindset shifts for cultivating healthy relationships. In the next chapter, we'll focus on repairing and rebuilding relationships impacted by insecure attachment, equipping you with powerful tools for fostering trust, empathy, and lasting connection.

Key Points to Remember:

- Overcoming avoidance requires embracing vulnerability and confronting fears of intimacy.

- Engaging in daily practices, like mindfulness and journaling, can significantly support emotional growth and self-awareness.
- Building trust with yourself and others is a gradual process, but each small step results in meaningful change.

A Short Message from the Author

Hi, are you enjoying the book thus far? I'd love to hear your thoughts!
Many readers do not know how hard reviews are to come by and how much they help an author.

Customer reviews

⭐⭐⭐⭐⭐ 1
5.0 out of 5 stars ▼

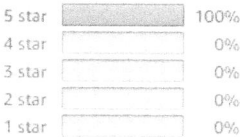

5 star	▓▓▓▓▓	100%
4 star		0%
3 star		0%
2 star		0%
1 star		0%

See all 1 customer reviews ›

Share your thoughts with other customers

Write a customer review

I would be incredibly thankful if you could take just 60 seconds to write a brief review on Amazon, even if it's just a few sentences!

Thank you for taking the time to share your thoughts!

CHAPTER 7: REBUILDING TRUST AND INTIMACY

"Trust is built when someone is vulnerable and not taken advantage of." – Bob Vanourek

WHAT DOES TRUST REALLY MEAN?

Before we dive into the process of rebuilding trust, it's essential to define what trust truly means in a relationship. Trust doesn't happen automatically; it's a conscious choice built over time through consistent actions, reliability, honesty, and emotional presence. It's earned, not demanded.

Trust doesn't require complete transparency regarding every single thought or action. Healthy boundaries and private thoughts are essential. Trust also doesn't necessarily mean sharing access to personal accounts, like banking details, social media, or devices. While some couples may choose to share these, trust is about faith and respect, not surveillance. With trust, there's no need to constantly check up on your partner because you know you can openly discuss any concerns.

SIGNS OF TRUST IN A RELATIONSHIP

Trust manifests in countless ways, both big and small, creating safety, reliability, and connection. Here are some key indicators:

1. Feeling Safe to Share Vulnerabilities

A key indicator of trust is the ability to be vulnerable with your partner without fear of judgment or rejection. Vulnerability means allowing your partner to see your true self—your fears, hopes, insecurities, and flaws. When trust is present, you can open up with confidence, knowing that your partner will respond with empathy and care.

What this looks like:

- Confiding in your partner about your fear of failure after a difficult day at work because you know they'll listen without belittling your feelings.
- Confessing a past mistake or insecurity and feeling supported rather than criticized.

2. Respecting Each Other's Boundaries

Boundaries are essential in any healthy relationship. They define what feels safe and comfortable for each partner, from physical touch to emotional intimacy, time, and communication. Respecting boundaries is a clear sign of trust, showing that each person values the other's comfort, autonomy, and well-being.

Here are some examples and real-life scenarios of respecting boundaries in relationships:

Physical Boundaries:

- **Example:** Asking for consent before initiating physical affection.
  - *Scenario:* You're in a new relationship, and your partner isn't a fan of public displays of affection. Instead of assuming they'll be okay with it, you ask, *"Would you be comfortable if I held your hand?"*
  - *Why it Matters:* It shows that you respect their comfort level rather than pushing them into something that makes them uneasy.
- **Example:** Respecting when your partner isn't in the mood for intimacy.
  - *Scenario:* Your partner has had a long, exhausting day and isn't in the headspace for physical closeness. Instead of taking it personally, you reassure them by saying, *"I understand. Let me know if you need space or if there's another way I can support you."*

- *Why it Matters:* It prevents guilt or pressure and builds trust, reinforcing that their needs will be honored.

Emotional Boundaries:

- **Example:** Honoring a partner's need for personal space or alone time without taking it as rejection.
  - *Scenario:* Your partner, who has an avoidant attachment style, asks for an evening alone to decompress after a stressful week. Instead of assuming they are pulling away from you, you say, *"I get that. Let's plan a night together later this week when you feel more recharged."*
  - *Why it Matters:* It reassures them that their need for space is respected and that it doesn't threaten the relationship.
- **Example:** Avoiding emotionally dumping on your partner without checking in first.
  - *Scenario:* You've had a frustrating day at work, and you're tempted to vent the moment your partner walks through the door. Instead, you pause and ask, *"Hey, I've*

had a rough day—do you have the energy to listen right now?"

- ○ *Why it Matters:* This shows respect for your partner's emotional capacity and fosters a reciprocal, supportive environment.

Time & Communication Boundaries:

- **Example:** Respecting a partner's preferred communication style and frequency.
  - ○ *Scenario:* You love texting throughout the day, but your partner prefers to focus on work and check in later. Instead of assuming they're uninterested, you discuss a middle ground: *"I know you're busy, so would you be okay if we checked in at lunch and then had a call in the evening?"*
  - ○ *Why it Matters:* It acknowledges differences in communication needs and prevents misunderstandings.
- **Example:** Not forcing difficult conversations at the wrong time.

- ○ *Scenario:* You want to talk about something serious, but your partner is visibly stressed and distracted. Instead of pushing them, you say, *"I know this is important, so let's talk when we're both in the right headspace. When would be a good time for you?"*

- ○ *Why it Matters:* It ensures that discussions happen when both partners are emotionally available, leading to more productive conversations.

3. Active Listening and Responding to Needs

Trust grows when partners actively listen to each other and address the needs or emotions that are shared. This involves more than just hearing words—it requires tuning in to your partner's emotional state, acknowledging their feelings, and showing that their needs matter.

What this looks like in action:

- If one partner shares, "I feel overwhelmed at work and could use some help at home," the other responds by asking, "What can I do to make things easier for you?"

- During a disagreement, one partner listens to the other's perspective without interrupting or invalidating their feelings.

4. Supporting Each Other in Times of Stress or Growth

Trust means knowing that your partner will be there for you—during the good times and challenges. It's about offering a steady presence and encouragement when life gets tough.

Examples of support:

- Providing reassurance when your partner is feeling anxious about a major life decision, like changing careers or moving to a new city.
- Stepping in to help with daily responsibilities when your partner is dealing with illness, grief, or burnout.

5. Maintaining Openness and Honesty

In a trusting relationship, both partners feel free to express their thoughts, feelings, and experiences without fear of criticism or being dismissed. This openness creates an environment where communication thrives.

What openness and honesty look like:

- Sharing concerns about the relationship, such as, "I've been feeling distant lately, and I want to figure out how we can reconnect."
- Being truthful about past mistakes or personal struggles, knowing that your partner will approach the conversation with compassion.

UNDERSTANDING THE LEVELS OF TRUST

Trust isn't built overnight—it evolves in stages as partners demonstrate reliability, emotional safety, and commitment through their actions. According to renowned relationship expert John Gottman, PhD, trust in a relationship develops in three key levels, each reflecting a deeper sense of security and connection.

1. Trust: The Foundation of Security

At this level, partners feel safe and secure enough to be vulnerable. They trust that their emotions, thoughts, and concerns will be met with understanding rather than judgment. There is mutual respect and reliability, but trust is still developing.

Example:

- You share something personal with your partner, like a past relationship struggle, and they listen without dismissing your experience.
- Your partner keeps small promises, like texting when they said they would or following through on plans.

Signs You're at This Level:

- ✓ You feel comfortable expressing your feelings, but there may still be some hesitation.
- ✓ You trust your partner to be honest and reliable, but deep emotional security is still growing.
- ✓ The relationship feels safe, but you haven't fully tested trust in high-stakes situations.

2. Trustworthy: Strengthening the Bond

This level of trust moves beyond basic reliability—partners show consistent dependability, even when it requires personal sacrifice. At this stage, trust becomes more resilient as both people prioritize the relationship's well-being over personal convenience.

Example:

- Your partner adjusts their schedule to support you when needed, such as taking time off work when you're sick.
- During conflict, instead of shutting down or withdrawing, both partners work through issues constructively, showing that trust is strong even in difficult moments.

Signs You're at This Level:

- ✓ You trust your partner to have your back in both small and big moments.
- ✓ You're both willing to compromise for the health of the relationship.
- ✓ When conflicts arise, trust remains intact, and there is no lingering fear of betrayal.

3. Commitment: The Deepest Level of Trust

At this highest level, partners don't just trust each other—they are fully committed to the relationship as a shared journey. They cherish the connection and actively choose each other every day.

Example:

- When life throws unexpected challenges—financial struggles, family conflicts, or personal hardships—both partners remain steadfast in supporting each other rather than considering an exit.
- Partners make long-term plans together, such as moving in, merging finances, or starting a family, with full confidence that they are in it for the long haul.

Signs You're at This Level:

- ✓ You never question whether your partner is in this with you—they consistently choose the relationship.

✓ You plan for the future together and trust that challenges will be faced as a team.

✓ Even when disagreements arise, there's no fear of abandonment—you both know your bond is solid.

Where Are You Now? *(Reflection Prompt)*

If you're in a relationship, consider which level of trust you and your partner are currently at.

- Do you feel secure in expressing your emotions?
- Do you trust that your partner will be there in difficult moments, not just easy ones?
- Are you both actively choosing and prioritizing the relationship?

If you're single, reflect on the level of trust you aspire to reach in future relationships.

- What actions can you take to build stronger trust in your next relationship?
- Are there past trust wounds you need to heal before fully committing to someone?

BUILDING TRUST IN EVERYDAY MOMENTS

No matter where you are in your journey, taking intentional steps toward deepening trust will create a more secure and fulfilling connection. Trust isn't just about big promises or grand gestures—it's built in the small, everyday interactions that shape the emotional foundation of a relationship.

Renowned relationship expert John Gottman, PhD, describes these moments as "Sliding Door Moments."

WHAT ARE "SLIDING DOOR MOMENTS"?

Gottman's research shows that trust is built (or broken) in seemingly ordinary moments—the ones where we have a choice:

- To turn toward our partner and strengthen the connection
- Or to turn away and miss an opportunity for closeness

These micro-moments define the emotional safety in a relationship. When partners consistently show up for each other in small ways, they create a reservoir of trust that helps sustain them through more significant challenges.

Examples of Sliding Door Moments

- **Recognizing and Responding**
  - Your partner looks upset after coming home from work. Instead of pretending not to notice, you say, *"You seem a little down—do you want to talk about what's on your mind?"* This simple acknowledgment makes them feel seen and valued.
- **Providing Support in Small Ways**
  - If your partner is nervous about a work presentation, you offer words of encouragement or ask how you can help. Even small gestures, like bringing them coffee or sending a supportive message, reinforce trust.
- **Choosing Connection Over Distraction**
  - Your partner reaches out for a hug or starts a conversation, but you're scrolling on your phone. Instead of

brushing them off, you pause, put your phone down, and engage—a small but meaningful moment of turning toward them.

Every time you turn toward your partner in these moments, you deposit trust into your relationship's "emotional bank account." Over time, these deposits create a strong foundation—one that carries you through tough conversations, misunderstandings, and life's inevitable challenges.

By recognizing Sliding Door Moments and choosing connection over avoidance, you strengthen the kind of deep, lasting trust that makes relationships truly thrive..

THE IMPACT OF AVOIDANCE ON TRUST

Avoidance can erode trust in subtle but powerful ways. By sidestepping difficult conversations or withdrawing emotionally, you may create barriers that leave your partner feeling unseen or unimportant. Even when avoidance is not meant to be deceptive, it can still foster misunderstanding, distance, and insecurity in a relationship.

How Avoidance Undermines Trust:

- **Creating Communication Breakdown:** Avoidance leads to a lack of open dialogue, making it harder to express needs, resolve issues, or build emotional closeness.
- **Fostering Emotional Distance:** When one partner pulls away during vulnerable moments, the other often feels neglected, unwanted, or emotionally isolated.
- **Leading to Perceived Secrecy:** Even when there is no ill intent, avoiding transparency can create suspicion or misinterpretation, making your partner wonder if something is being hidden.

I remember when my friend Tommy learned this lesson the hard way. He wasn't the kind of guy to lie to his wife, but he was the type to avoid uncomfortable conversations.

One night, Tommy stayed late at work, but instead of telling his wife, Sarah, that he was grabbing a drink with a coworker afterward, he chose to say nothing. He figured it wasn't a big deal—after all, it was just a quick drink, and he didn't want to deal with any unnecessary questions.

But when he got home later than expected and acted a little distant (as he often did when feeling guilty about something minor), Sarah picked up on it immediately. When she casually asked how his night went, Tommy gave vague responses, making her more suspicious. She wasn't upset about him having a drink—she was upset because it felt like he was hiding something.

That one small act of avoidance led to a tense night, unnecessary anxiety, and lingering doubt. Later, Tommy admitted that Sarah wouldn't have minded if he had just been upfront about his plans. But his avoidance made her feel excluded as if there was something he didn't want her to know.

This is how avoidance erodes trust—not necessarily through deception, but through omission, withdrawal, and lack of transparency. Even when it's done to "keep the peace" or "avoid unnecessary drama," it often has the opposite effect, making a partner feel more insecure, not less.

Avoidance might feel like a short-term solution, but it can create long-term damage to trust. True emotional security comes from facing difficult conversations with honesty, even when it feels uncomfortable.

REBUILDING TRUST

Rebuilding trust requires addressing these patterns head-on and committing to a more open, honest way of relating. It requires patience, humility, and mutual commitment. Here are key strategies:

1. Listen and Validate

When trust is broken, the hurt partner needs to feel heard. Resist the urge to defend yourself or minimize their pain. Instead:

- Acknowledge your actions and their impact: "I understand that my behavior hurt you, and I'm deeply sorry."

- Reflect their emotions back to them: "It sounds like you felt unimportant when I didn't follow through on what I promised."

Deep listening helps the hurt partner feel seen and understood, creating a foundation for healing.

2. ATTUNE to Emotions (Gottman)

- **A**ttend to your partner's emotions.
- **T**urn toward them instead of away.
- **T**ry to understand their perspective.
- **U**nderstand their emotional needs.
- **N**on-defensively respond with empathy.
- **E**mpathize with their experience.

3. Take Consistent Action

Rebuilding trust isn't just about words—it's about demonstrating reliability over time. Follow through on your promises, no matter how small, to show your partner that they can depend on you.

4. Change the Dynamic

Sometimes rebuilding trust means breaking old patterns. Replace defensive reactions with vulnerability. Instead of withdrawing, lean into difficult conversations. This change can foster a sense of security and connection. For example:

- Instead of criticizing your partner, express your own emotions: "I felt hurt when you didn't tell me about your plans. Can we work on being more transparent?"
- Replace avoidance with engagement. If conflict arises, lean into the discomfort and address it directly.

5. Cultivate Empathy

Empathy is the ability to step into your partner's experience, understand their emotions, and respond in a way that makes them feel heard, valued, and safe. When trust has been damaged—whether through avoidance, emotional withdrawal, or miscommunication—empathy becomes a crucial tool for repair.

Empathy validates their feelings, even when you don't fully understand or relate to them. By showing that you genuinely care about their emotions, you help rebuild a sense of security and openness in the relationship.

How to Cultivate Empathy in Relationships:

- Listen with Intent
- Resist the Urge to Fix or Defend
- Put Yourself in Their Shoes
- Use Small Gestures to Show You Care

Empathy counteracts the effects of avoidance by replacing distance with understanding. It tells your partner:

- *"Your emotions matter to me."*
- *"I am willing to see things from your perspective."*
- *"You can trust me to hold space for your feelings, even when difficult."*

COMMUNICATING WITHOUT FEAR

Open and honest communication is crucial for trust and intimacy; it bridges the chasm of broken trust.

When trust is damaged, communication takes on a heightened importance. It's no longer just about sharing daily events; it's about being vulnerable, taking responsibility, and showing a genuine commitment to rebuilding the connection. This requires a shift from defensive communication patterns to a more constructive, trust-building communication style.

Here's how communication contributes to rebuilding trust:

1. **Transparency and Accountability:** When trust is broken, the hurt partner often feels a deep sense of uncertainty and insecurity. Transparent communication alleviates these feelings by providing clarity and demonstrating accountability. This means:

   o **Openly acknowledging your role in the breach of trust:** Avoid minimizing, justifying, or deflecting blame. Take full ownership of your actions and their impact. For example, instead of saying, "It wasn't that big of a deal," try, "I understand that my actions hurt you deeply, and I take full responsibility."

- o **Providing honest and complete information:** Be straightforward and honest in your responses, even if the truth is uncomfortable to share. Transparency builds trust by showing that you're not hiding anything.

- o **Being consistent in your communication:** Inconsistency creates further distrust. Be consistent in your words and actions to prove you can be counted on.

2. **Emotional Vulnerability and Empathy:** Restoring trust requires demonstrating emotional vulnerability and empathy. This means:

- o **Sharing your own feelings and regrets:** Expressing genuine remorse and sadness about the hurt you've caused shows that you understand the consequences of your actions. For example, "I feel terrible that I hurt you, and I truly regret what I did."

- o **Actively listening to your partner's pain:** Create a safe space for your partner to express their feelings without being interrupted or judged. Validate their emotions and show that you understand their perspective. For example, "I can hear how much this has hurt you, and I want to understand what you're going through."

- o **Expressing a desire to understand and make amends:** Show your partner that you're committed to understanding their experience and making amends for your actions. This reflects your willingness to put in the work to rebuild the relationship.

3. **Future-Oriented Communication and Reassurance:** Rebuilding trust also involves communicating about the relationship's future and providing reassurance. This means:

- o **Clearly expressing your commitment to the relationship:** Reassure your partner of your desire to rebuild trust and continue the relationship.

- ○ **Discussing concrete steps to prevent future breaches of trust:** Collaboratively develop strategies to prevent similar situations from happening again. This shows that you're taking proactive steps to protect the relationship.
- ○ **Being patient and understanding:** Rebuilding trust takes time. Be patient with the process and understand that your partner may need ongoing reassurance and support.

Shifting from Self-Protection to Trust-Building Communication:

The key shift is moving away from communication patterns driven by self-protection (avoidance, defensiveness, minimizing) and toward communication that actively builds trust (transparency, vulnerability, empathy, reassurance). This requires conscious effort and a willingness to step outside your comfort zone, but the rewards—a stronger, more secure, and more intimate relationship—are well worth the effort.

BEST PRACTICES FOR REBUILDING TRUST

Rebuilding trust requires more than good intentions—it calls for deliberate actions and mutual effort. Both partners should cultivate a supportive, respectful dynamic while actively engaging in practices that foster empathy, understanding, and emotional connection. Below are practical strategies and exercises to strengthen your bond and create a foundation for lasting security in your relationship.

CULTIVATE MUTUAL RESPECT

Mutual respect is the bedrock upon which trust, intimacy, and long-term happiness are built. It creates a safe and nurturing environment where both individuals can flourish.

Here's how to cultivate mutual respect in your relationship:

1. Show Appreciation Daily:

Showing appreciation isn't just about saying "thank you." It's about acknowledging and appreciating your partner's efforts, both big and small.

213

- **Instead of assuming your partner knows you're grateful:** Verbalize it! "I really appreciate you making time for me today, even though I know you had a lot going on."
- **Acknowledge the everyday gestures:** "Thanks for handling the grocery run—it really helped me out."
- **Show appreciation for emotional support:** "I felt truly heard when you listened to me vent earlier—thank you for being there."
- **Use physical touch and affectionate gestures:** A quick hug, a gentle touch, or a genuine compliment can go a long way in expressing appreciation.

Consistent appreciation reinforces the positive aspects of your relationship. It shows your partner that their contributions are valued and encourages them to continue investing in the relationship.

2. Honor Boundaries as Acts of Love:

Respecting your partner's boundaries isn't about giving in or sacrificing your own needs. It's about demonstrating trust and valuing their autonomy.

- **If your partner needs alone time:** Instead of interpreting it as rejection, acknowledge it: "I understand you need some time to recharge—let me know when you're ready to reconnect."
- **If your partner is hesitant to discuss a topic:** Respect their pacing: "I don't want to pressure you, but whenever you feel comfortable talking about it, I'm here to listen."
- **If they seem overwhelmed:** Offer reassurance instead of pushing: "I can tell this is a lot for you right now. Let's take a break and revisit it later if that feels better."

Honoring boundaries strengthens trust and demonstrates that you value your partner's well-being above your own immediate needs.

3. Celebrate Differences as Unique Strengths:

Every relationship will have differences in personality, communication styles, and emotional responses. Instead of viewing these differences as obstacles, celebrate them as unique strengths.

- **Embrace diverse perspectives:** If your partner is more introverted and you thrive in social settings, find a middle ground that honors both your needs.
- **Respect different processing styles:** If your partner needs time to process emotions while you prefer immediate resolution, acknowledge and respect their pace.
- **Learn from each other's strengths:** If one of you is a planner and the other is more spontaneous, use that to your advantage.

When partners learn to appreciate and even leverage their differences, they create a dynamic where both individuals feel valued for who they truly are.

PRACTICE GRATITUDE

Gratitude shifts your focus from what's missing to what's meaningful in your relationship. It's easy to overlook the small, thoughtful things your partner does, but acknowledging these actions reinforces positive feelings and strengthens your bond.

Gratitude not only boosts your partner's confidence but also helps you both focus on the positive aspects of your connection.

PRIORITIZE UNDERSTANDING

Misunderstandings are inevitable in any relationship, but they don't have to lead to disconnection. By prioritizing understanding, you create a space where both partners feel heard and validated.

How to Foster Understanding

- Ask Open-Ended Questions: Instead of making assumptions, ask questions like: "Can you help me understand how you're feeling about this?" or "What would feel most supportive to you right now?"
- Reflect What You Hear: Summarize your partner's words to ensure you've understood their perspective. For instance, say: "It sounds like you're feeling overwhelmed because of work deadlines. Is that right?"

- Validate Their Experience: Even if you don't fully agree, acknowledge their feelings. "I can see why that would make you feel frustrated."

Prioritizing understanding helps de-escalate conflicts and reinforces your partner's sense of emotional safety.

INTENTIONAL EXERCISES FOR CONNECTION

In addition to cultivating respect, gratitude, and understanding, engaging in intentional activities can help couples deepen their connection and foster trust.

1. Gratitude Lists

Gratitude lists are a simple but powerful way to focus on the positives in your relationship.

How to Do It:

- Each partner writes a list of things they appreciate about the other. These can include specific actions ("I love how you always make me coffee in the morning") or qualities ("Your kindness inspires me").

- Set aside time to share your lists during a quiet moment, such as after dinner or before bed.

Why It Works: Hearing what your partner values about you deepens emotional intimacy and reinforces the strength of your bond.

2. Shared Journaling

A shared journal serves as a safe space for both partners to express their thoughts, feelings, and reflections.

How to Do It:

- Use a physical notebook or a digital app where both partners can write entries.
- Take turns adding to the journal, sharing insights about your day, your emotions, or your relationship.

Example Prompts:

- "What's something I did this week that made you feel loved?"

- "What's a goal you're working toward, and how can I support you?"

Why It Works: Shared journaling encourages open communication and provides a written record of your journey together, fostering connection and mutual understanding.

3. Conflict Resolution Practice

Conflicts are inevitable, but resolving them constructively strengthens trust and intimacy.

How to Do It:

1. Choose a Recent Disagreement: Select a conflict you haven't fully resolved.
2. Discuss Calmly: Sit down together in a distraction-free environment and agree to approach the conversation with curiosity rather than defensiveness.
3. Share Perspectives: Take turns explaining your viewpoint without interruption. Use "I" statements to express your feelings, such as, "I

felt hurt when we canceled our plans without discussing it first."

4. Collaborate on Solutions: Brainstorm ways to address the issue in a way that honors both perspectives. For example, "Next time, let's decide together before making changes to our plans."

Why It Works: By practicing conflict resolution in a structured, empathetic way, you develop skills to navigate future disagreements with greater ease and trust.

BLENDING PRACTICES AND EXERCISES INTO DAILY LIFE

While these strategies and exercises are valuable individually, their true power lies in consistent practice. Weaving them into your daily routine creates a dynamic where trust, empathy, and intimacy are continually nurtured.

Tips for Integration

- Create Rituals: Establish weekly rituals, such as sharing gratitude lists every Sunday or setting aside time for shared journaling once a week.

- Check-In Regularly: Dedicate time to discuss how you're feeling about the relationship and areas for growth.
- Celebrate Progress: Acknowledge the small wins in your relationship, like resolving a disagreement or completing an exercise together.

CASE STUDY: ELLA AND DAVID

Ella and David had been married for 10 years when they hit a rough patch. Ella often felt neglected because David tended to withdraw during stressful times. On the other hand, David felt burdened by Ella's need for reassurance, interpreting it as criticism.

Through couples counseling, they began to understand their patterns. David learned to communicate his need for space without shutting Ella out, and Ella practiced expressing her feelings without blame. Over time, their relationship transformed. They now describe their connection as "stronger than ever," built on mutual respect, patience, and a shared commitment to growth.

Rebuilding trust isn't a one-time fix—it's a daily commitment to lean in, listen, and show up for each other. It's about saying, *"I see you, I hear you, and I'm here for you,"* even when it feels difficult.

Trust transforms relationships from fragile connections into resilient bonds. As you move forward, ask yourself:

- *What level of trust are we at?*
- *What steps can I take to strengthen our connection?*

Recap: Trust is the foundation of every meaningful relationship. Rebuilding it requires consistency, patience, and intentional effort.

We examined strategies for fostering trust, including listening deeply, validating emotions, and attuning to your partner's needs. You learned how "sliding door moments" can strengthen the emotional bond between you and your partner. We also discussed the importance of repairing ruptures in relationships and navigating conflict with empathy and openness.

Key Points to Remember:

- Trust is built through small, consistent actions that show reliability and care.
- Repairing trust requires deep listening, vulnerability, and taking responsibility for your mistakes.
- Emotional intimacy thrives when both partners feel safe to express themselves without fear of judgment.

As you reflect on this chapter, consider the areas where trust has been challenged in your relationships. What steps can you take to rebuild trust and foster greater emotional closeness?

CHAPTER 8: LIVING BEYOND THE WALLS

"Growth is never by mere chance; it is the result of forces working together." – James Cash Penney

When Christina first walked into my office, she described her life as "living in a fortress." She had built walls so high and so thick that no one could get in—not even the people who cared about her the most. She told me she felt safe behind those walls, but also lonely, stuck, and disconnected. Christina had spent years protecting herself from hurt, but in doing so, she had also shut out love, joy, and the possibility of real connection.

225

One day, Christina decided she was tired of feeling trapped in her own fortress. She began to dismantle those walls, brick by brick. It wasn't easy—there were moments of fear, doubt, and discomfort—but with each step, she felt lighter, freer, and more alive. She started to let people in, little by little, and discovered that vulnerability wasn't a weakness—it was the key to deeper relationships and a more fulfilling life.

This chapter is about what it means to live beyond the walls—to break free from the self-imposed barriers that hold us back from connection and personal growth. Growth, both personal and relational, is a continuous journey, not a destination. It's about adapting, evolving, and embracing change, even when it feels uncomfortable.

"Walls" can take many forms: negative thought patterns, limiting beliefs, fear of vulnerability, avoidance behaviors, or unmet needs. Living beyond them means:

- **Embracing vulnerability and connection:** Choosing to engage with others authentically, even when it feels risky.

- **Challenging limiting beliefs:** Reframing negative self-perceptions and embracing a growth mindset.

- **Prioritizing self-awareness and emotional regulation:** Understanding your needs and managing your reactions in healthy ways.

- **Committing to ongoing growth:** Recognizing that personal and relational development is a lifelong process.

Christina's story is a reminder that the walls we build don't have to define us. With courage, self-compassion, and intentional effort, we can dismantle them—one brick at a time—and step into a life of deeper connection and fulfillment.

STRATEGIES FOR ONGOING DEVELOPMENT

The growth journey can feel daunting, but the right tools and resources make it both empowering and achievable. Here are some strategies to nurture continuous development:

- **Expanding Your Knowledge and Perspectives:** Learning new information and exploring different viewpoints broadens your understanding of yourself and relationships. This can involve:

- o Reading books and articles on relevant topics (communication, emotional intelligence, attachment).
- o Listening to podcasts or attending workshops.
- o Taking courses on mindfulness, boundary setting, or related areas.

- **Cultivating Self-Reflection and Mindfulness:** Self-awareness is crucial for identifying patterns and making intentional choices. Practices like:
  - o **Journaling:** Reflect on experiences, emotions, and aspirations. Consider prompts like: What limiting belief am I ready to let go of? What progress have I made in my relationships?
  - o **Meditation and Mindfulness:** Focus on the present moment to observe thoughts and emotions without judgment.

- **Spending Time in Nature:** Find quiet time for introspection and processing thoughts.

- **Building a Supportive Community:** Connecting with others who share your commitment to growth provides encouragement, accountability, and diverse perspectives. This can involve:
  - Joining online or in-person support groups or forums.
  - Attending workshops or meetups.
  - Connecting with supportive friends and family.

- **Seeking and Integrating Feedback:** Honest feedback from trusted individuals can reveal blind spots and accelerate growth. This can involve:
  - Asking for specific feedback from friends, family, or a therapist.
  - Approaching feedback with openness and a desire to learn.

- **Celebrating Progress and Embracing Imperfection:** Growth is about progress, not perfection. One of the biggest shifts my clients have made is learning to acknowledge and celebrate their achievements, no matter how small. Over the years, I've worked with many individuals who struggled with avoidant attachment, and the ones who made the most lasting changes were those who actively recognized their progress—instead of focusing on what they hadn't mastered yet.

I've seen clients break lifelong patterns of avoidance by making small but meaningful shifts in their relationships. Whether it's expressing emotions more openly, engaging in deeper conversations, or choosing connection over withdrawal, these moments deserve recognition. Acknowledging progress reinforces motivation and keeps you moving forward. This can involve:

- o Reflecting on milestones in a journal.
- o Rewarding yourself for reaching goals.
- o Sharing your progress with others.

Many clients felt discouraged early on, thinking they weren't "doing enough." But they realized how far they had come when they started tracking and celebrating their efforts.

We all have an inner voice. Sometimes, it encourages us and offers support, but other times, it can be a harsh critic, whispering doubts and fears that hold us back. These negative thoughts and limiting beliefs act like invisible walls, keeping us from truly connecting with others and living fulfilling lives. They're often so ingrained that we don't even notice them, silently shaping our perceptions and reactions. Identifying and challenging these inner critics is a crucial step in living beyond those walls and building secure connections.

Recognizing the Whispers of the Inner Critic:

These negative thoughts rarely shout; they tend to whisper, subtly influencing our decisions and interactions. They often take predictable forms:

- **Catastrophizing: The "What If" Game:** This is when your mind jumps to the worst possible outcome, even when there's no real evidence. It's the "what if I open up and they reject me?" or "what if I try something new and fail miserably?" game.

This kind of thinking fuels anxiety and prevents us from taking risks, especially in relationships.

- **Black-and-White Thinking: The All-or-Nothing Trap:** This is seeing things in extremes—everything is either perfect or a complete disaster, with no middle ground. In relationships, this might sound like, "If we have one argument, it means we're not meant to be" or "If I'm not always happy, the relationship is failing." This leaves little room for the normal ups and downs of any connection.

- **Personalization: Taking Everything Personally:** This is the tendency to believe that everything negative that happens is somehow your fault. If your partner is in a bad mood, you might automatically assume it's because of something you did, even if it has nothing to do with you. This can lead to unnecessary guilt and self-blame.

Challenging the Inner Critic's Narrative:

Once you start recognizing these negative thought patterns, you can begin to challenge their validity. It's similar to having a conversation with that inner critic, but instead of letting it dictate the narrative, you take initiative to ask some tough questions:

- **"Is this thought actually based on evidence, or is it just an assumption?"** Our negative thoughts are often based on fears and insecurities rather than concrete facts.
- **"What's a more balanced and realistic way to look at this situation?"** Instead of jumping to the worst-case scenario, consider other possibilities.
- **"If a friend were having this thought, what would I say to them?"** We're often much kinder and more compassionate to our friends than we are to ourselves. Try to extend that same kindness to your own inner critic.

Reframing Negative Thoughts: Turning the Volume Down:

Here are some examples of how to reframe common negative thoughts:

- **Instead of:** "If I show vulnerability, I'll get hurt."

- o **Try:** "Vulnerability can deepen my connection with others, and while it might be uncomfortable at times, I can handle it."
- **Instead of:** "I'm not good enough to be loved."
  - o **Try:** "I'm worthy of love and connection, just as I am. I have strengths and weaknesses, just like everyone else."
- **Instead of:** "If I rely on someone, they'll let me down."
  - o **Try:** "It's okay to ask for support. I can choose to build trust gradually with people who show they are reliable."

OVERCOMING LIMITING BELIEFS

Limiting beliefs are like deeply ingrained stories we tell ourselves about who we are and what we're capable of. These stories typically stem from past experiences, but they don't have to define our future. Here are some ways to rewrite these harmful narratives:

- **Trace the Origin:** Begin by tracing the roots of your limiting belief. Where did it come from? Was it something someone told you as a child? Did it develop after a painful experience? Understanding the source of the belief can help you see it in a new light.

- **Challenge Its Validity:** Is this belief universally true? Are there exceptions? Are there times when this belief hasn't held true?
- **Replace It with an Affirmation:** Create a new, positive belief that reflects your potential for growth and connection. This might take time and repetition, but with consistent effort, you can start to rewrite your story.

CONVERTING GUILT INTO PERSONAL GROWTH

Guilt. It's that uncomfortable feeling in the pit of your stomach, the nagging voice that reminds you of something you did (or didn't do) that you now regret. It can be a heavy burden, a constant reminder of our imperfections. But what if we shifted our perspective on guilt? Instead of viewing it as a punishment, what if we could see it as a valuable signal, a signpost pointing us toward growth and deeper connection?

Guilt often arises when we realize we've acted in a way that contradicts our values or have hurt someone we care about. It's a signal that something needs our attention. The key is to avoid getting stuck in a cycle of self-blame and shame. Instead, we can use guilt as an opportunity for self-reflection and positive change.

Think of it this way: Guilt is like a check engine light in your car. While it's not a pleasant sight, it conveys something important. Ignoring guilt won't make the problem go away; in fact, it might worsen things. The same applies with guilt. Ignoring it can lead to resentment, defensiveness, and further damage to our relationships.

Owning It, Not Dwelling in It:

The first step in transforming guilt is to acknowledge it with complete honesty. This means:

- **Facing the Music:** Admit to yourself and, if necessary, to the other person, what happened. Avoid minimizing your actions or making excuses. Saying something like, "I realize I wasn't there for you when you needed me, and I'm truly sorry," is much more powerful than saying, "I was busy, but..."

- **Reflecting on the Lesson:** Once you've acknowledged your actions, ask yourself: "What can I learn from this? What could I have done differently? How can I prevent this from happening again?" This is where the real growth happens, as it allows you to extract valuable lessons from your experience.

Taking Action: From Regret to Repair:

Guilt becomes a catalyst for growth when we pair it with action. It's not enough to feel bad; we need to take concrete steps to make amends and demonstrate our commitment to change. This involves:

- **Offering a Sincere Apology:** A genuine apology is more than just saying "I'm sorry." It involves acknowledging the specific hurt you caused, expressing remorse, and taking responsibility for your actions. It's about showing that you understand the impact of your behavior on the other person.
- **Making Amends:** This can range from a simple gesture of kindness to a more significant change in behavior. The goal is to show you're committed to

doing better through your actions. For example, if you have a habit of canceling plans at the last minute, making amends might mean making a conscious effort to prioritize your commitments and clearly communicate if something comes up.

- **Focusing on Future Behavior:** The most important part of this process is focusing on how you intend to act differently in the future. This shows that you've learned from past experiences and are dedicated to personal growth.

Example:

Imagine you forgot an important anniversary and feel incredibly guilty. Instead of beating yourself up about it, you could:

1. **Acknowledge it:** "I completely forgot our anniversary, and I feel awful. I know this was important to you, and I'm so sorry."
2. **Reflect:** "I realize I've been so focused on work lately that I haven't been prioritizing our relationship. I need to be more mindful of important dates and make more time for us."

3. **Take action:** "I've booked a special dinner for us this weekend to make it up to you. And moving forward, I'm going to set reminders on my phone for important dates and make a conscious effort to be more present in our relationship."

By turning guilt into a learning opportunity and taking concrete steps to make amends, we not only repair the damage we've caused but also strengthen our relationships and build a stronger sense of self. We transform guilt from a burden into a bridge to deeper connection and personal growth.

RECOGNIZING PERSONAL NEEDS

Understanding your own needs is fundamental to living beyond avoidance. These needs—emotional, physical, and relational—are the driving force that makes us feel secure, valued, and truly alive. When we neglect them, we become depleted, resentful, and more likely to fall back into self-protective patterns. Conversely, when we honor them, we create a foundation for thriving.

The Landscape of Human Needs:

239

It's beneficial to think of needs in different categories:

- **Emotional Needs:** These relate to our inner world and how we experience and process feelings. They include:
  - **Feeling understood and validated:** This means having others acknowledge and accept our emotions, even if they don't necessarily agree with them. It's the feeling of being seen and heard.
  - **Emotional safety and support:** This involves feeling safe to express vulnerability without fear of judgment, criticism, or rejection. It's the assurance that there are people you can turn to when you're struggling.
  - **Autonomy and independence:** This is the need to feel in control of your life and make your own choices. It's about having the freedom to pursue your interests and maintain a sense of individuality within relationships.

- **Physical Needs:** These are the needs of our bodies, which directly impact our emotional and mental well-being. They include:
  - **Physical touch and affection:** This can range from hugs and cuddles to more intimate forms of physical connection. It's about establishing a sense of closeness and bonding with others.
  - **Rest and relaxation:** This is essential for recharging our batteries and preventing burnout. Regular downtime helps us unwind from the stresses of daily life, giving us a chance to rejuvenate our minds and bodies.
  - **Health and well-being:** This includes things like proper nutrition, exercise, and adequate sleep. Taking care of our physical health has a profound impact on our emotional state.
- **Relational Needs:** These pertain to how we interact with others and the kind of connections we seek. They include:
  - **Quality time and connection:** The focus here is spending meaningful time

with loved ones, engaging in activities you enjoy together, and creating shared experiences. It's not just about being in the same room; it's about being present and engaged.

- ○ **Open communication and mutual respect:** This involves honest and respectful communication, active listening, and valuing each other's perspectives. It's about creating a safe space for open dialogue and vulnerability.

- ○ **Trust and intimacy:** The ability to feel safe in being vulnerable with others and trusting that they will be there for you creates a deep sense of connection.

Tuning Inward: Reflecting on Your Experiences:

A powerful way to identify your needs is to reflect on times when you felt most at peace, connected, or fulfilled. Ask yourself:

- What contributed to those feelings?
- What was happening in my life at that time?

- What needs were being met?

For example, if you felt most at peace during a quiet weekend alone reading a book, it might indicate a need for solitude and time to recharge. If you felt most connected during a deep conversation with a friend, it might highlight a need for open communication and emotional intimacy.

Articulating your needs is not selfish but an act of self-care and a vital step in building healthy relationships. Clearly communicating your needs empowers you to create relationships and environments that support your growth and well-being, propelling you to live beyond the walls of avoidance.

As you continue on this path, remember to be patient with yourself. Celebrate each small victory and approach the future with curiosity, courage, and hope. Beyond the walls lies a world of opportunity—step into it with confidence and an open heart.

Recap: The final chapter invited you to fully embrace a life of connection, authenticity, and secure attachment. Living beyond the walls means breaking

243

free from negative thinking, challenging limiting beliefs, and enjoying the freedom that comes with self-awareness and emotional growth.

We discussed practical strategies for maintaining this transformation, including recognizing your personal needs, building healthy relationships, and committing to continuous growth. The chapter emphasized that this journey doesn't end here—it's a lifelong process of learning, adapting, and deepening your connections. Celebrating your progress and acknowledging your growth are essential milestones of this enriching path.

Take time to reflect on how far you've come and the tools you've gained throughout this book. What steps will you take today to live beyond the walls and create the life and relationships you envision?

CONCLUSION

"We don't have to do all of it alone. We were never meant to." – Brené Brown

As we reach the end, take a moment to reflect on the courage it took to begin this process. This book isn't intended to be a one-sided conversation or a list of instructions; it's meant to be a shared experience that encourages you to confront your fears, challenge patterns, and adopt a new way of living.

Let me share a story of transformation that reminds us of what's possible when we step beyond the walls. Sarah came to me years ago, her heart guarded by high, thick walls. Fiercely independent and accomplished, she felt isolated, avoiding conflict and emotional

245

conversations, silently worrying she was incapable of truly loving or being loved. "I don't know how to let someone in without feeling like I'm losing myself," she confessed.

Together, we began the work. It wasn't easy. Sarah dealt with the discomfort of confronting long-ignored emotions and practiced vulnerability in small ways, sharing fears and needs with her partner for the first time. While she faced setbacks and reverted to old patterns, she persisted, fueled by hope.

Months later, a quiet smile graced her face. "I feel different," she said. "I'm not perfect, but I don't feel like I'm running anymore. And for the first time, I'm letting someone run *toward* me."

Sarah's story may resonate with you. You, too, have begun breaking down walls that once felt protective but kept you from the connection you deserve. Recognizing this shift is a sign that you're already on the path to change.

Throughout this book, we've explored key principles:

- **Understanding Avoidant Attachment:** Recognizing that these tendencies are protective mechanisms rather than flaws, and that change is possible
- **The Strength in Vulnerability:** Discovering that vulnerability is courage, not weakness, opening the door to deeper intimacy and trust.
- **The Power of Communication:** Exploring strategies for open, honest, and empathetic dialogue—the cornerstone of healthy relationships.
- **Building and Rebuilding Trust:** Understanding how trust is built through consistent actions and how it can be repaired after breaches.
- **Living Beyond Avoidance:** Identifying ways to challenge limiting beliefs, recognize personal needs, and live authentically.
- **Committing to Ongoing Growth:** Embracing personal and relational development as a lifelong journey.

Reaching this point is a testament to your courage and commitment. Transformation is within your grasp, and you have the power to create the life and relationships you deserve.

Along the way, there may have been moments of discomfort when self-reflection felt overwhelming, or vulnerability seemed too intense. But it's through these struggles that you've experienced growth. You've proven to yourself that transformation is achievable and that you have the power to create the life and relationships you deserve.

Your growth has a ripple effect. Every act of empathy, vulnerability, or trust strengthens your connections and inspires those around you.

This book was a starting point, a spark igniting your journey. Now, it's time to take action:

- **Reflect:** Revisit the lessons that resonated most and find ways to integrate them into your daily life.
- **Practice:** Engage in small acts of vulnerability—sharing feelings, setting boundaries, and asking for support.

- **Celebrate:** Acknowledge your progress. Every step outside your comfort zone creates a new pattern.
- **Persist:** Transformation isn't linear. Setbacks are opportunities for learning and growth.

Imagine yourself in the future, no longer confined by walls but living a life of connection and authenticity. Your relationships are grounded in trust, your voice is clear, and your heart is wide open. You navigate challenges with grace, leaning into discomfort rather than retreating.

You now have the tools to create this life. Each day is an opportunity to deepen your relationships and strengthen your connection to yourself and others. While your journey is unique, it contributes to a broader movement of empathy and understanding.

Carry these lessons with you. View every conversation as an opportunity for deep listening. Let each challenge be a chance to grow. In every relationship, show up wholeheartedly, armed with courage and compassion.

The journey doesn't end here—it begins. Step forward confidently, knowing you can create the love and connection you deserve. You've done the work. Now it's time to live beyond the walls.

One more thing!

If you enjoyed this book and found it helpful, I'd be very grateful if you'd post a short review on Amazon. Your support does make a difference, and I read all the reviews personally so I can get your feedback and make this book even better. I love hearing from my readers, and I'd really appreciate it if you leave your honest feedback.

Thank you for reading!

BONUS CHAPTER

I would like to share a sneak peek into another one of my books that I think you will enjoy. The book is titled ***"The Path to Secure Attachment: Transforming Anxious and Avoidant Patterns into Secure Relationships, and Leveraging Attachment Theory for Healthy Relationships and Emotional Intelligence."***

Do you yearn for deeper connection, but find yourself trapped in cycles of frustration and longing?

"The Path to Secure Attachment" is your guide to transforming your relationships, breaking free from unhealthy patterns, and embracing the fulfilling love you deserve.

Building upon the insights of *"Anxious Attachment and Avoidant Detachment,"* this book delves into the heart of secure attachment – the cornerstone of healthy, thriving relationships. Discover how to cultivate the safety, trust, and balanced emotional connection that fosters lasting love.

Your Transformation Starts Here

Understand the profound impact of your earliest experiences on your adult relationships. Uncover the neurobiology of attachment: how your brain forms bonds and how this impacts the way you navigate intimacy. Learn how to recognize your own attachment style and those of others, unlocking a deeper understanding of your behaviors and relationship dynamics.

This book is your roadmap to transform insecure attachment patterns into a secure, balanced state. Develop the skills essential for fulfilling connection:

- **Master Effective Communication:** Express your needs with clarity and compassion, and learn to truly listen to your partner.

- **Cultivate Emotional Intelligence:** Decode your emotions and those of your partner, creating a space for understanding and empathy.

- **Build Unshakeable Trust:** Overcome past hurts and learn to rely on your partner for support and comfort.

- **Nurture Self-Compassion:** Embrace your strengths and weaknesses, offering yourself the same kindness you extend to loved ones.

The Benefits Extend Far Beyond Your Romantic Life

Secure attachment is the foundation for strong connections across all areas of your life. Learn how to:

- **Strengthen Friendships and Family Bonds:** Apply the same principles of empathy and clear communication to deepen all your relationships.

- **Become a Secure Base for Your Children:** Raise emotionally healthy children by providing them with the secure attachment they need to thrive.

- **Enhance Workplace Collaboration:** Build stronger rapport with colleagues, approach conflict with confidence, and cultivate a sense of belonging within your team.

- **Improve Your Relationship with Yourself:** Develop greater self-awareness, treat yourself with compassion, and set healthy boundaries.

- **Boost Overall Well-being:** Experience reduced stress, increased resilience in facing challenges, and a greater sense of personal fulfillment.

AVOIDANT ATTACHMENT STYLE RECOVERY

- **Navigate the World with Confidence:** Secure attachment fosters a sense of safety and security, allowing you to explore new experiences, take healthy risks, and approach challenges with greater ease.

Don't settle for a life of missed connections and unfulfilled relationships. "The Path to Secure Attachment" empowers you to break free from the past and build the future you desire – a future filled with resilient love, mutual support, and deep, lasting connection.

Seize this opportunity for growth. Buy your copy today and embark on a journey towards secure, fulfilling relationships.

Enjoy this free chapter!

We all yearn for secure, supportive connections—they're the foundation upon which we thrive. This journey promises new insights into the intricate world of relationships and deeper self-understanding. Whether the prequel, Anxious Attachment and Avoidant Detachment, inspired deeper introspection and sparked your curiosity, or this is your first exploration of attachment theory's impact on relationships, your engagement with these pages is vital. This sequel builds upon the foundation of the prequel, expanding your understanding and offering new insights, deeper explorations, and practical guidance for nurturing secure, healthy relationships. *The only way to live is to grow - And that journey of growth includes how we form and nurture relationships.*

Understanding attachment is an ongoing journey of self-discovery and growth. "In the prequel, I explored the patterns of anxious and avoidant attachments, revealing how these early bonds shape our adult relationships. Now, we focus on the cornerstone of resilient relationships: secure attachment. This book will empower you with practical tools to foster security and stability in all your relationships. While the prequel exposed the challenges of insecure attachment, this book provides the path toward healing and change.

Secure attachment is more than just a theory; it embodies a state of emotional balance, mutual respect, and understanding. It means feeling comfortable asking for support, working through conflict calmly, and celebrating each other's successes. It's about forming connections that aren't only enduring but also supportive and enriching. As we embark on this new phase of our journey together, we'll explore the principles of secure attachment, understand its implications for our daily lives, and learn how to cultivate and maintain these healthy bonds.

This book is structured to be both a reflection of

your journey and a guide for your path ahead. Each chapter builds upon the insights and lessons from the prequel, providing a deeper understanding of attachment styles and offering practical strategies for nurturing secure relationships. Whether you're seeking personal growth, healing from past relationships, or looking to strengthen your current bonds, this book is designed to meet you where you are and guide you forward.

As you begin this exploration, remember that each page, concept, and strategy contributes to a larger journey—one of understanding, growth, and connection. This book isn't just a set of pages to be read; it's a journey to be experienced, a path to be walked, and your story of transformation.

Together, we'll delve into secure attachment, understanding its theory and the practical, life-changing ways it can manifest in our lives and relationships. Let's turn the page – a new chapter of possibility and transformation begins.

Think of this book as a dialogue with your innermost self. These pages mirror your experiences, aspirations, and the intricate dynamics of your relationships. This is where your journey intersects with the collective narrative of those striving for secure, meaningful, and enriching connections. This book is your companion, guide, and confidant as you navigate the intricacies of building nurturing and enduring relationships.

Prepare to be challenged, inspired, and transformed. Remember that every insight gained is a step forward. Every reflection deepens your understanding. Every strategy applied is a tool for forging stronger, more resilient, and more fulfilling bonds. This is an expansion of your horizons, a deepening of your insights, and a celebration of the journey that each of us is on— toward understanding ourselves, our attachments, and the web of relationships that we weave throughout our lives.

As we focus on nurturing secure attachment, let's revisit the foundational concepts of attachment theory explored in the prequel. This theory—a cornerstone of understanding emotional bonds—provides invaluable insights into the intricacies of human relationships. It's about how we relate to others, and understanding the deep-seated patterns that guide our interactions and shape our emotional landscape of trust and vulnerability.

Attachment theory, pioneered by John Bowlby and expanded by Mary Ainsworth and others, shows us how the bonds formed between a child and their primary caregivers set the stage for future relationship dynamics. These early interactions establish patterns for how individuals perceive themselves and others, influencing their sense of security, their ability to form and maintain emotional bonds, and their response to intimacy and dependency.

261

The theory categorizes attachment into four distinct styles:

1. **Anxious Attachment (sometimes referred to as "Preoccupied"):**
   - Develops from inconsistent caregiving and emotional availability.
   - Results in adults who seek high levels of intimacy, approval, and responsiveness from partners, often fearing rejection or abandonment.

2. **Avoidant Attachment (sometimes referred to as "Dismissive"):**
   - Arises from caregivers who are emotionally unavailable or unresponsive.
   - Leads to adults who are self-sufficient to the point of pushing others away, often prioritizing independence over intimacy.

3. **Disorganized Attachment (sometimes referred to as "Fearful-Avoidant"):**

- Usually stems from trauma or severe inconsistency in caregiving.
- Results in adults who desire close relationships but find it hard to trust or depend on others completely.

4. **Secure Attachment:**
   - Originates from consistent, responsive caregiving.
   - Leads to adults with a positive view of themselves, their partners, and their relationships.
   - Characterized by comfort with intimacy as well as independence to create balanced and healthy relationships.

Understanding these styles is crucial as they provide a framework for examining our own behaviors and preferences in relationships. Recognizing one's own attachment style can be deeply illuminating, offering explanations for feelings and behaviors that previously seemed confusing. It empowers individuals to navigate their relationships more mindfully, understand their own needs, and empathize with those of their partners.

We'll revisit these attachment theory concepts by viewing them as building blocks for the chapters ahead. They serve as the framework through which we delve into the intricacies and principles of secure attachment, offering a comprehensive and enlightened foundation for the practical strategies and insights presented in this book.

In exploring secure attachment, we embrace the evolving nature of relationships, knowing that challenges, life changes, and growth are all part of the journey. Secure attachment isn't about achieving a state of perfection; it's about cultivating a sense of balance, understanding, and mutual respect. It's about creating a foundation of security within ourselves. This security radiates outward, enriching all our relationships.

We'll delve into the interplay between self-awareness, empathy, and communication – essential elements for secure, healthy relationships. This exploration isn't just theoretical; it's practical and deeply personal. It's about bringing the principles of secure attachment to life and making them a living reality in your day-to-day interactions.

Whether you're seeking healing, growth, or to help others, this book offers a structured path with insights, reflections, and exercises to support you every step of the way. It's intended to be a living document in your life that you can consult, reflect upon, and draw insights from over time. Here's how to maximize the value you get from it:

1. **Engage Deeply for Maximum Impact**

   - Read actively, not mindlessly. Engage with the material by considering how it applies to your personal experiences. Reflect on the concepts and theories presented and relate them to your own life.

2. **Explore, Reflect, and Grow**

- Take your time with each chapter, allowing the ideas to sink in. Reflect on how the information might change your understanding of your past interactions and how it might influence your future ones. Use the book as a journal of sorts, making notes in the margins or in a separate notebook where you can write down thoughts, feelings, and revelations.

3. **Put Your Learning into Action**

- Gradually implement the insights and strategies you learn in your life. Change is a process; lasting transformation occurs through consistent, intentional practice over time. Focus on one concept or strategy at a time, and observe how it influences your relationships and your perspective on attachment.

4. **Find Support and Share Insights**

- Use the book as a conversation starter with friends, family, or a therapist. Discussing your insights and challenges with others can provide new perspectives and deepen your understanding of the material.

5. **Your Evolving Companion**

- Your relationship with this book should evolve alongside you. Different sections may become more relevant or have new meanings as you grow and change. Make it a habit to revisit parts that struck a chord with you or that you found particularly challenging, and see if your new experiences shed new light on them.

6. **Embrace Patience on Your Journey**

- The journey to understanding and fostering secure attachment in your life isn't linear. It will have its ups and downs – days when insights feel clear, and days when old patterns resurface. Approach this journey with patience and compassion for yourself. Change takes time, and self-growth is a continuous, often nonlinear process.

The insights and strategies within these pages hold the greatest potential for transformation when reflected upon and applied to your unique life experiences. The heartfelt application of these ideas will foster the growth and development of more secure, enriching relationships in your life. View each chapter as an opportunity to deepen your understanding of yourself and your relationships. Let this book be a companion and a guide as you navigate the complex yet rewarding path toward secure attachment and relational fulfillment. It recognizes that the pursuit of secure attachment isn't confined to a particular relationship status or life stage. Whether you're single, immersed in the complexities of dating, deeply rooted in a long-term partnership, or fostering familial and platonic bonds. The principles of secure attachment are universally applicable, offering the potential for transformation at every stage of life.

The journey toward secure attachment is as individual as it is universal. While each person's journey is unique – shaped by past experiences and individual goals – our underlying need for connection and growth binds us together.

For those who are single, this book sheds light on the patterns that have defined past relationships and offers a framework for building future connections with intention and clarity. It gives you the knowledge to understand your attachment style, identify red flags early on, and lay the groundwork for partnerships built upon mutual growth and support.

For individuals in relationships, the insights within these pages provide a deeper understanding of your own and your partner's attachment styles. This knowledge is powerful—it transforms communication, aids conflict resolution, and strengthens the bonds of intimacy and trust. It's about nurturing a relationship that's both enduring and deeply fulfilling, offering a safe space for both individuals to grow and flourish.

Parents will find in this book a valuable resource for shaping their children's communication styles, conflict resolution skills, and capacity for trust. The principles of secure attachment, when introduced early in life, can cultivate the seeds for future relationships that are healthy, resilient, and fulfilling. It's about creating an environment that fosters emotional intelligence, empathy, and a deep sense of security from the earliest stages of development.

Furthermore, this book extends its reach beyond

individual relationships to the broader community. It sparks the creation of supportive networks where individuals can share experiences, offer support, and grow together. It's a call to build a community that values emotional intelligence, mutual respect, and collective well-being.

As you progress through this book, remember that the path to secure attachment, though personal, echoes the universal human quest for connection, understanding, and growth. Each step forward not only enriches your own life, but ripples outward - contributing to a world where everyone feels capable of healthy, supportive, and transformative relationships.

Embrace the journey that this book invites you to embark upon. Let it guide you toward deeper, more meaningful connections in every facet of your life. Through individual growth and shared understanding, we can cultivate a world where secure attachment isn't just an ideal but a lived reality, where every relationship is an opportunity for mutual support, profound connection, and enduring growth.

Get your full copy today!

BEST SELLERS BY RICHARD BANKS

Assertiveness Training: Learn How to Say No and Stop People-Pleasing by Establishing Healthy Boundaries

The Keys to Being Brilliantly Confident and More Assertive: A Vital Guide to Enhancing Your Communication Skills, Getting Rid of Anxiety, and Building Assertiveness

The Art of Active Listening: How to Listen Effectively in 10 Simple Steps to Improve Relationships and Increase Productivity

How to Deal With Stress, Depression, and Anxiety: A Vital Guide on How to Deal with Nerves and Coping with Stress, Pain, OCD and Trauma

How to Deal with Grief, Loss, and Death: A Survivor's Guide to Coping with Pain and Trauma, and Learning to Live Again

Develop a Positive Mindset and Attract the Life of Your Dreams: Unleash Positive Thinking to Achieve Unbound Happiness, Health, and Success

How to Stop Being Negative, Angry, and Mean: Master Your Mind and Take Control of Your Life

For the Full Book Listing go to

https://author.to/RichardBanksBooks

REFERENCES

Asarnow, J. R. 2021. Dialectical Behavior Therapy (DBT): Skills for Emotional Regulation.

Beck, A. T. 1976. Cognitive Behavioral Therapy (CBT): Reframing Negative Thought Patterns.

Bowlby, J. 1988. *A Secure Base: Parent-Child Attachment and Healthy Human Development.* Basic Books.

Gottman, J., & Silver, N. 2011. *The Science of Trust: Emotional Attunement for Couples.* W. W. Norton & Company.

Gottman Institute. (n.d.). *Sliding Door Moments.* Retrieved from www.gottman.com.

Johnson, S. M. (2004). Emotionally Focused Therapy (EFT): Attachment-Focused Interventions for Couples.

Johnson, S. M. 2008. *Hold Me Tight: Seven Conversations for a Lifetime of Love*. Little, Brown Spark.

Levine, A., & Heller, R. (2010). *Attached: The New Science of Adult Attachment and How It Can Help You Find – and Keep – Love*. TarcherPerigee.

Mikulincer, M., & Shaver, P. R. (2007). Attachment in Adulthood: Structure, Dynamics, and Change. *Journal of Personality and Social Psychology, 92*(5), 884–896. doi:10.1037/0022-3514.92.5.884.

Naragon-Gainey, K., McMahon, T. P., & Park, J. (2017). Emotional Regulation and Resilience: A Meta-Analysis of Strategies for Psychological Well-Being. *Clinical Psychology Review, 57*, 61–75. doi:10.1016/j.cpr.2017.08.002.

Simply Psychology. (n.d.). Attachment Styles and Their Impact on Relationships. Retrieved from www.simplypsychology.org.

Spring, J. A. (2004). *How Can I Forgive You? The Courage to Forgive, the Freedom Not To.* Harper Perennial.

The Human Connection Blog. (2022). Avoidant Attachment: Signs and Healing. Retrieved from www.thehumanconnectionblog.com.

Van Edwards, V. (n.d.). *Reading Emotions in Relationships* [Video]. Retrieved from www.scienceofpeople.com.

Verywell Mind. (n.d.). Repression as a Defense Mechanism. Retrieved from www.verywellmind.com.

Printed in Great Britain
by Amazon